M000226793

The Family Worship Guide

A Handbook for the Christian Home

Darren T. Williamson

Keledei
PUBLICATIONS

An Imprint of Sulis International Press
Los Angeles | London

The Family Worship Guide: A Handbook for the Christian Home
Copyright ©2020 by Darren T. Williamson. All rights reserved.

Except for brief quotations for reviews, no part of this book may
be reproduced in any form or by any electronic or mechanical
means, including information storage and retrieval systems,
without written permission from the publisher. Email:
info@sulisinternational.com.

ISBN (print): 978-1-946849-78-6
ISBN (eBook): 978-1-946849-79-3

Published by Keledei Publications
An Imprint of Sulis International
Los Angeles | London

www.sulisinternational.com

Contents

Acknowledgements

Many people encouraged and enabled the writing of this guide. I am thankful to the Keizer Church of Christ family and its leadership for graciously allowing me some time of sabbatical during the summer of 2016. During that period, I was able to bring together this guide. Original versions of this booklet derived from a Bible class at Keizer in 2010 on raising godly children. The monthly worship guides following that series were the product of feedback from that class and dialogue with then Associate Minister, Erik Granberg, and Secretary, Julie Boatner. They both provided helpful comments on the earlier versions of the worship guide. As well, the Keizer Wednesday night singing class unknowingly helped with the selection of the hymns in the book when they picked their "top 20" hymns one night. That data found its way into the resource page.

I also want to express a debt of gratitude to the various Christian couples who inspired our family's experience of family worship. Specifically, John Wyatt (and his late wife, Betty) of Vancouver, Washington. This lovely older couple not only showed my family hospitality during a family road trip but welcomed us into their daily time of family worship. Their example provided us with a tangible image of what family worship looks like when it is an integral part of the home's rhythms, even when the kids are grown and gone. Another couple, Paul and Julie Hinds of Tigard, Oregon, made a powerful impact on our spiritual life together. Their presentation on raising godly children at a Cascade College Kingdom Builder seminar and sidebar discussions gave us ideas and practical advice that are blessing our children today. Speaking of our kids, they each played a role in parts of the guide. Besides being the guinea pigs for many of the experiments we've tried in family worship over the years, they contributed to parts of this guide as it came together in its final form. My wife Melody offered excellent advice about content, style, and issues related to final editing. Without her help and encouragement this guide probably would have remained simply an idea and an outline, rather than a completed project. I also want to thank my good friend and colleague in ministry, Mike Soto, who provided valuable feedback on content. My English Major daughter enjoyed critiquing the manuscript and thereby made it much more readable. Of course, the opinions, judgments, and inevitable errors in the text are all mine.

Soli deo Gloria
Darren T. Williamson

Embracing the Call to Family Worship

Christianity in North America at the beginning of the 21st century is facing a crisis like it has never seen before. Rampant secularism, progressive liberalism, and the general moral breakdown of society has greatly impacted the Church. Poll after poll reveals that North Americans are turning their back on the Christian faith and the fall away rate for young people with a semi-Christian upbringing is staggering. Thoughtful and observant Christians don't need polls and statistics to convince them that the Church is in trouble; they see it in their dwindling churches and the increasing number of young people who abandon the faith of their parents as they enter their late teens and twenties. To be sure, Christ is still King and head of the Church, and He is working even through this moment in time to nurture and strengthen His body. Nevertheless, it is appropriate for believers to ask what we should do in the face of this crisis.

This handbook is a call to rediscover and implement the old and biblical practice of family worship, a joy producing discipline that will radically blunt the fall away rate, encourage the development of multigenerational disciples, and strengthen the core of Christian families throughout the body of Christ. Embracing the long-neglected practice of family worship requires rethinking how we view the children of the church--that is, children raised in Christian families. Several attitudes toward children of the Church and youth ministry need to change (such as over-segregating children from the larger church community and over-booking their schedules), but the most basic perspective that needs to change is the expectation that someone else, usually a paid children's minister or youth minister, will disciple my child. Rather than expecting paid professionals to raise children in the Lord, we should be calling, equipping, and holding parents accountable for that most important obligation.

The basic conviction underlying this handbook is that Christian parents have a special and profound calling, a mission from God that He has equipped and ordained them to accomplish in the world. That calling is to disciple their children faithfully and instruct them in the ways of Christ. This conviction doesn't take away from the church's role in helping shape a child's faith; rather, it puts the Church's role in proper perspective. Our congregation makes a big deal about babies born to members. Babies receive a special visit from one of their ministers and are prayed over and blessed within a day or so of their arrival into this world. A month or two later, we introduce this new baby to the church family and one of our Elders prays a special blessing over the child and the parents. At an important moment in the blessing, he gently but solemnly exhorts the parents to raise the child to "know, love, and serve Jesus Christ." The church then stands and receives a similar exhortation to help the child "know, love, and serve Jesus Christ." At this powerful moment, everyone is reminded that the church family has a critical role to play in the spiritual growth of that child. From the nursery attendants and Sunday school teachers to the Deacons and Elders and everyone in between, we all help shape that child's faith. The church community makes a critical contribution to raising that child in Christ, especially in situations where the ideal family situation has been shattered or when a child comes into the life of the church apart from parental involvement.

No matter how important the Church's part is, however, the greatest and most important role in shaping that child's faith has been entrusted to her parents by God. As Christians witnessing a crisis of falling away, we must return and embrace this fundamental concept if we are to see the next generation continue in faithfulness. The best and most basic means for Christian parents to heed and obey this calling is to ensure that family worship is an established practice in their homes.

What is family worship? It is not "worship of the family," as if we make the nuclear family an object of worship. Christ's Church is the new family, the family of God on a spiritual level, and has a higher status. Jesus told his disciples that some of them would have to abandon their earthly families in order to follow him, receiving instead a thousand-fold blessing of spiritual relatives that circles the globe and exists in the heaven-lies. Having said that, the Bible still views the Christian family unit as the most important and basic human community, and it is at that level that faith must be exercised and nurtured. Second, family worship is not a replacement for assembling with the broader church, or just something that happens when the normal Sunday assembly is canceled (such as in a snowstorm or pandemic). Some also wrongly view "family worship" as something they do when their other commitments (such as Sunday morning sports or vacations) or narrow-mindedness (sectarian home church) keep them from a regular gathering with a larger Christian community. Family worship, correctly understood, does not compete with the Sunday assembly but complements it.

At its most basic level, family worship is the regular gathering of the family to worship God and receive instruction in the Christian faith. In the past, family worship was a common and established practice of dedicated Christians, attested to in the writings of the early Church, the sixteenth-century Reformers, the Puritans, and prominent leaders in the American Restoration Movement. Family worship today, however, is rarely practiced and many dedicated Christians have no understanding or experience of it. The busyness of modern life and breakdown of the family make it difficult for many to even eat a meal in the same place, let alone spend time together in worship. But, for the reasons outlined above, this must change. Christian parents must again take up the call to raise their children in the

Lord, and a fundamental part of fulfilling that calling is family worship.

This handbook is designed to inspire and equip Christian parents to take up that call by making family worship an established part of a family's routine. The first chapter provides a rationale for family worship by showing that the Bible envisions the home as the primary a place where God is worshiped and faith is established, reveals that Christian history bears witness to the importance of the family in transmitting faith, and argues that common sense teaches us that parents must play the prominent role in their children's religious development. The second chapter calls attention to the great blessings that family worship will bring and that it is worth the effort and discipline that it takes to incorporate it into the family's life. It also offers helpful encouragement for how a family can get started, while remaining sensitive to the fact that many families have little or no experience with family worship. New Christians with young children will especially need help implementing this practice, as many of their mentors in the faith have no experience of it themselves. The third chapter lays out the four basic components of Family worship and provides practical guidelines about how to conduct meaningful worship in the home. The fourth chapter offers detailed resources, including quarterly and weekly guides, Bible & topical discussion questions, Bible reading plans, song lists, and other tools.

There are many different specific ways that family worship can happen, and this guide does not claim to represent the only valid approach. However, it is a time-tested and simple method that has yielded tangible and good spiritual fruit in my family. The statistics and polls about the departure of Christian children from the faith can be discouraging, especially when we realize that there is little an individual can do to reverse those larger trends. We can each do our part in our corner of the Church, in our own families and in our children's lives. If we each tend our own spiritual garden, while not neglecting to help those around us who need it, we can reverse these trends and bring honor and glory to God. Family worship is one simple, yet profound and effective, place to start.

The Reason for Family Worship

Before addressing the "how" of family worship, it is important to talk about the "why." Implementing new practices into our family rhythms and patterns requires conviction about the reason for it. We will see in this chapter that there are excellent biblical, historical, and practical reasons family worship should be a regular feature of the Christian home.

The Biblical Basis for Family Worship

The most important reason to embrace family worship is that parents have a biblical mandate to personally pass on faith to their children. Consistently throughout the entire Bible, the home is viewed as the central place where faith is transmitted to the next generation of believers.

In the Old Testament, the home is the essential place where the pivotal events of Israel's history are commemorated and taught. The identity of the Israelites as God's chosen people was solidified when he rescued them from slavery in Egypt. God struck down the first-born of the Egyptians but spared the Israelites who smeared blood over the doorposts of their homes. This event is commemorated annually as the Feast of Passover and is accompanied by the Feast of Unleavened bread, two celebrations based in individual homes and calling for personal instruction by parents.

Regarding the Passover, Moses told God's people, "…you shall keep this service. And when your children say to you, 'What do you mean by this service?' you shall say, it is the sacrifice of the LORD's Passover…" (Exodus 12:26; ESV[1]). Further in the section, Moses provided more instruction about the Passover, specifically that the lamb or goat "shall be eaten in one house; you shall not take any of the flesh outside the house, and you shall not break any of its bones" (Exodus 12:46;). The home is ground zero for remembering the Passover. As well, the accompanying Feast of Unleavened Bread is to be celebrated in the home and explained to children directly by parents. Moses said, "You shall tell your son on that day, 'It is because of what the LORD did for me when I came out of Egypt. And it shall be to you as a sign on your hand as a memorial between your eyes, that the law of the LORD may be in your mouth" (Exodus 13:8-9). Finally, fathers must explain the consecration of the firstborn to their own children. He wrote, "And when in time to come your son asks you, 'What does this mean?' you shall say to him, 'By a strong hand the Lord brought us out of Egypt, from the house of slavery" (Exodus 13:14).

---

[1] Unless otherwise noted, all quotations from Scripture come from the English Standard Version.

From the beginning, then, God commanded the Israelites to make their homes places of instruction. Most religions have a consecrated priesthood and sacred temples and shrines that serve as the primary place for religious instruction. Biblical faith acknowledges those things, but it centers instruction in the home. Parents, specifically fathers, are commanded to personally instruct their children in the grand story of God's deliverance. They are not told to bring their children to the priests for instruction or rely on the professional religious classes. Parents are told to explain to their own children the great deeds of Yahweh when He delivered them from bondage.

Years later, after the dramatic events of Mount Sinai and the subsequent lapse into sin and forced wandering in the desert, the Law came to the people once again. As a new generation of Israelites prepared to enter the Promised Land, God reiterated the essential task of parents in communicating His will to the next generation. One of the most famous passages in the Bible is known as the Shema, and Jesus identifies it as the greatest commandment of the Law. It reads:

> Hear, O Israel: The LORD our God, the LORD is one. You shall love the Lord your God with all your heart and with all your soul and with all your might. And these words that I command you today shall be on your heart. You shall teach them diligently to your children, and shall talk of them when you sit in your house, and when you walk by the way, and when you

> lie down, and when you rise. You shall bind
> them as a sign on your hand, and they shall be
> as frontlets between your eyes. You shall write
> them on the doorposts of your house and on
> your gates. (Deuteronomy. 6:7-9)

This striking and succinct statement of monotheistic belief was foundational for the Israelites, but it was alien and unknown to the cultures around them and required constant communal reinforcement. When it comes to how this conviction and the rest of the Law should be communicated to each generation, it cannot be any clearer. The family is where these convictions are established, transmitted, and reinforced. Unlike other religions, God's law is not just talked about by the priests or by elders of the community on special feast days and festivals. It is part of the everyday fabric of the family's existence. It is to be performed diligently, not accidentally or lackadaisically. Diligently means purposefully, thoughtfully, consistently, and creatively. God's Word is to be discussed in every part of family life: hanging out in the house, driving down the road, at bedtime, at meals. It even finds its way into the furniture and symbolic spaces in the house, indicating the priority and focus of the family. The mandate is clear: God's people must teach their children His law and do so in creative and intentional ways in the home.

Further in the section, fathers are again told to attentively teach their children the reason for all the laws that Israel is to keep.

When your son asks you in time to come, 'What is the meaning of the testimonies and the statutes and the rules that the Lord our God has commanded you?' then you shall say to your son, 'We were Pharaoh's slaves in Egypt. And the Lord brought us out of Egypt with a mighty hand. And the Lord showed signs and wonders, great and grievous, against Egypt and against Pharaoh and all his household, before our eyes. And he brought us out from there, that he might bring us in and give us the land that he swore to give to our fathers. And the Lord commanded us to do all these statutes, to fear the Lord our God, for our good always, that he might preserve us alive, as we are this day. And it will be righteousness for us, if we are careful to do all this commandment before the Lord our God, as he has commanded us.' (Deuteronomy 6:20-25)

The clear sense of the entire passage is that Israel's faithfulness is dependent upon a diligent and purposeful attention to the law and that the family is the primary place where this is to happen. Interestingly, it is the child who asks and the parent who is to respond with a thorough answer. As will be noted later, the genius of this method of transmitting faithfulness lies in the fact that for parents to teach their children, they must know the law themselves. A father cannot explain and teach something to his children that he does not personally understand. Many parents who have brushed up on history, math, science, and literature to help their child with homework understand this all too well. As the saying goes, "to teach is to learn." This dynamic may be one of the reasons God put the burden of religious instruction on parents. Unfortunately, the history of Israel's unfaithfulness suggests that they failed to heed this fundamental command to teach their own children. The Psalmist reflects on the importance of this command, saying:

> He established a testimony in Jacob and appointed a law in Israel, which he commanded our fathers to teach to their children, that the next generation might know them, the children yet unborn, and arise and tell them to their children, so that they should set their hope in God and not forget the works of God, but keep his commandments. (Psalm 78:5-7)

As the Psalmist emphasizes in this passage, when a father or mother personally and diligently teaches their children about the Lord and His Word, the following generations are impacted in a positive way. To put it another way, when I take the time to worship and pray with my children and teach them God's Word, I'm not only impacting their faith, but the faith of my unborn grandchildren. Parents who obey the command to teach their children to place their hope in God, remember his deeds, and obey His Word, will positively influence many generations to come. Alternatively, when parents do not diligently disciple their children and they fall away after leaving home, someone else will have to evangelize their adult children and their grandchildren.

Other passages in the Old Testament attest to the critical importance of teaching and instruction of children.

Each time, the assumed primary instructors are the parents. Proverbs, the storehouse of spiritual and practical wisdom for God's people, begins with a solemn exhortation to youth to pay close attention to their parents' teaching:

> Hear, my son, your father's instruction and forsake not your mother's teaching, for they are a graceful garland for your head and pendants for your neck. (Proverbs 1:8-9)

> My son, if you receive my words and treasure up my commandments with you, making your ear attentive to wisdom and inclining your heart to understanding; yes, if you call out for insight and raise your voice for understanding, if you seek it like silver and search for it as for hidden treasures, then you will understand the fear of the Lord and find the knowledge of God. (Proverbs 2:1-5)

> My son, do not forget my teaching, but let your heart keep my commandments, for length of days and years of life and peace they will add to you. Let not steadfast love and faithfulness forsake you; bind them around your neck; write them on the tablet of your heart. So you will find favor and good success in the sight of God and man. (Proverbs 3:1-4)

> Hear, O sons, a father's instruction, and be attentive, that you may gain insight, for I give

> you good precepts; do not forsake my teaching.
> When I was a son with my father, tender, the
> only one in the sight of my mother, he taught
> me and said to me, "Let your heart hold fast my
> words; keep my commandments, and
> live." (Proverbs 4:1-4)

There are more examples in Proverbs and other sections of the wisdom literature, but these few selections demonstrate that personal parental instruction of children is a biblical mandate. Obviously, if Proverbs urges children to heed parental instruction, it assumes parents will actually be teaching their children. Much of Proverbs is considered practical wisdom and includes the kinds of things any good parent would teach their children, but this cannot be used as an excuse to avoid religious instruction. There is no sharp distinction between spiritual and practical wisdom in the Bible. Fearing God and honoring Him is the basis of all knowledge and wisdom (Proverbs 1:7), whether it involves knowledge and wisdom about everyday speech, social relationships, or how to stay faithful to God's will for your life. These are all things to be taught and modeled by parents in formal and informal settings alike, and family worship provides the ideal place for this instruction.

When we turn to the New Testament, it's no surprise to find that the Apostles built upon this theme in their writings on family. Paul's exhortation to Christian fathers is a succinct expression of everything taught in the Old Testament about maintaining multigenerational faithfulness. He writes, "Fathers, do not provoke your children to anger, but bring them up in the discipline and instruction of the Lord" (Ephesians 6:4). Paul addresses both the tone and content of teaching and who is to do the instructing. Fathers are to raise children through instruction in the faith, but they are to do it in a way that does not antagonize or embitter them. The passage points to two kinds of teaching: one that is focused on behavior or thinking that needs correction (discipline) and another that is more positive in nature (instruction) and carried out on a regular and consistent basis. The phrase "of the Lord" captures a whole host of doctrine about the God of the Bible and His will for our lives. Regardless of the specific kind of instruction envisioned, Paul's words plainly mean that parents are personally responsible for a child's spiritual and moral development as the God-ordained primary teachers of their children.

The New Testament's teaching about the qualifications for Church leaders is also instructive. One qualification for leading the church as an Overseer is a home life characterized by marital fidelity, order, godliness, and faithful children. Referring to a prospective Overseer, Paul writes, "He must manage his own household well, with all dignity keeping his children submissive, for if someone does not know how to manage his own household, how will he care for God's church?" (I Timothy 3:4-5; see also Titus 1:5-9). If a man is going to shepherd, teach, encourage, bless, and watch over the souls of the broader community, there needs to be evidence that he did the same for his family. The family is a microcosm of the church and looking closely at how a man did in that sphere tells you whether he can shepherd the larger church family.

Fathers are singled out in Scripture as responsible for educating their children in Christ, but this doesn't negate the important role of godly mothers. Paul specifically commends Timothy's mother and grandmother for teaching his young protege the Holy Scriptures from his childhood (II Timothy 1:5; 3:15). In Acts 16, we learn that Timothy's father was a Greek and therefore not capable or willing to instruct his son in the faith; instead, Timothy received that teaching from the spiritual women in his life. They raised Timothy in Christ so successfully that he sacrificed greatly to go on the missionary journeys with Paul. Later, Timothy was entrusted with spiritual care of the church in Ephesus, one of the largest Christian communities at the time and plagued with false teaching and mismanagement. Timothy's story should be a source of strength and inspiration for all mothers, especially Christian moms raising their children without a husband.

The ideal Christian marriage presented in the New Testament is a spiritual relationship that spills over into the rest of family life. Paul and Peter both envision husbands and wives as forming a complete unity in Christ, having an intimate bond in the Lord that is bolstered by shared times of prayer and worship in the assembly and in the home. Their physical intimacy should only be interrupted with mutual agreement for a short period of devotion to Christ (I Corinthians 7:5). Their closeness of relationship is compared to the relationship between God the Father and the Son (I Corinthians

11:1-16) and involves mutual respect and love, lest the relationship with God is hindered (I Peter 3:7). The beautiful imagery of spiritual relationship between husband and wife in Ephesians 5:22-33 supports a vision of home life that involves regular family worship as a natural and obvious part of living out the obedience of faith.

The dominant image used for the Church in the New Testament is the family. Paul tells Timothy to put affairs in order in the church in Ephesus so people will know how to conduct themselves in the "household of God" (I Timothy 3:15). Repeatedly, the Church is compared to a household and family, with God as the head (I Corinthians 4:1; Galatians 6:10; Ephesians 2:19). Besides that, the early Church met in homes for worship and that environment alone communicated the importance of the home for religious instruction. The home was naturally viewed as a place where worship occurred, not just when the whole assembly came together, but also during the normal routines of family life.

Without a doubt, the biblical model for transferring the faith to the next generation is the home and the family. We are seeing a large fall away rate among our current generation and the utter absence of a truly biblical worldview among Christian young people. Why? Because many Christian parents have neglected this essential biblical command. Most have assumed that someone more educated, more spiritual, or more efficient would teach their children about God. But this negligence is having a negative effect on our children and it must be stopped. It is time to return to a biblical model that faithful Christians in times past have embraced, a model that helps parents obey the command to disciple their own children: family worship.

The Historical Precedent for Family Worship

A brief survey of Christian history reveals that something like family worship has been encouraged and practiced throughout the life of the Church, especially at times when Christianity is successfully making genuine disciples of Christ. Remember, Christians in the early centuries were religious minorities fighting for their new-found faith in a hostile environment. The surrounding culture understood the importance of family for religion. Leaving behind the traditional gods of your ancestors was a form of family treason. The typical family in the Greco-Roman context had a private altar in the home where family members offered small acts of worship to local deities or ancestors in addition to their public religious duties at civic shrines and temples. The same is true of Jews who came to believe that Jesus was the promised Messiah. Converts to Christianity would find it natural and obvious to worship Christ in both the assembly of believers and their private homes.

The Early Church

While there is no extended discussion of family worship in the years immediately following the first century church, other influential sources illustrate the priority of the home in the early centuries for Christian instruction. One example comes from the second century Shepherd of Hermas. After contending that God earnestly desires the conversion of the reader's family, the speaker provides an earnest appeal:

> Do not be negligent, but be of good courage and strengthen your family. For as a smith shapes the object he desires by striking it with a hammer, so also a righteous word spoken daily overcomes all wickedness. Do not cease then to admonish your children, for I know that if they repent with their whole hearts, their names will be inscribed with those of the saints in the book of life.[2]

Vigilance and hopefulness are to characterize parents' approach to children's faith, a principle repeated in other second-century writings known as the Apostolic Fathers. The Didache counsels readers, "Do not neglect your responsibility to your son or daughter, but from their youth you shall teach them to revere God" (4.9); Polycarp instructs the Philippians to "educate their

---

[2] Hermas, *Visions* I.3.1-2. Quoted in Everett Ferguson, *Inheriting Wisdom. Readings for Today from Ancient Christian Writers* (Peabody, MA: Hendrickson Publishing, 2004), 13.

children in the fear of God" (4.2), and I Clement exhorts, "Let us rear our young in the fear of God...Let our children have a Christian training" (21.6-8). Immediately following the first century, the Christian material on the family exhorts parents to instruct their children daily in the Word of God.[3]

The later Church Fathers continued to emphasize religion in the home. Tertullian, a prolific Christian writer from North Africa around the beginning of the third century, penned a fascinating booklet to his wife in which he describes the power and importance of a godly Christian marriage. Making the case for Christian marriage, Tertullian extolls the virtues of sharing faith together:

> Together they pray, together prostrate themselves, together perform their fasts; mutually teaching, mutually exhorting, mutually sustaining. [8] Equally (are they) both (found) in the Church of God; equally at the banquet of God; equally in straits, in persecutions, in refreshments...Between the two echo psalms and hymns; and they mutually challenge each other which shall better chant to their Lord. Such things when Christ sees and hears, He joys.[4]

---

[3] Quotes from the *Early Christian Fathers, The Library of Christian Classics* (Philadelphia: The Westminster Press, 1953).
[4] Tertullian, *To My Wife*, Book 2, Chapter 8. Accessed April 4, 2018 at http://www.tertullian.org/anf/anf04/anf04-13.htm#P836_199870 .

Tertullian's emphasis on a unified faith in marriage is based on the conviction that this godly marriage will produce a context in which faith will be transmitted to the next generation.

John Chrysostom, nicknamed the "Golden Mouth" for his eloquence, is one of the most famous preachers in the history of Christianity, and his spiritual and eloquent sermons challenged, delighted, and taught thousands of Christians in the late 4th Century. He devoted an entire treatise to helping Christian parents personally shape their children's character and faith. In his view, Christian parents are like artists entrusted with precious material. Chrysostom writes,

> To each of you fathers and mothers I say, just as we see artists fashioning their paintings and statues with great precision, so we must care for these wondrous statues of ours. Painters when they have set the canvas on the easel paint on it day by day to accomplish their purpose. Sculptors, too, working in marble, proceed in a similar manner; they remove what is superfluous and add what is lacking. Even so must you proceed. Like the creators of statues do you give all your leisure to fashioning these wondrous statues for God. And, as you remove what is superfluous and add what is lacking, inspect them day by day, to see what good qualities nature has supplied so that you will increase them, and what faults so that you will eradicate them. And, first of all, take the great-

est care to banish licentious speech; for love of this above all frets the souls of the young. Before he is of an age to try it, teach thy son to be sober and vigilant and to shorten sleep for the sake of prayer, and with every word and deed to set upon himself the seal of the faith.[5]

Chrysostom emphasizes that parents should make a constant, daily effort to shape their children's faith, training them to value prayer above sleep and eventually guiding them toward the waters of baptism, the "seal of the faith." He also describes the value of Christian singing, writing, "Let their words be giving thanks, solemn hymns; let their discourse ever be about God, about heavenly philosophy." Above all, Chrysostom urges parents to personally teach their children the stories of the Bible at home around the dinner table, particularly stories that shape moral character.[6] Chrysostom's view of multigenerational faithfulness hinges on the home as the ideal biblical place for Christian instruction.

In two other writings, Chrysostom exhorts families to make Christ the center of the home, to be "little churches" where God's name is praised. Commenting on Ephesians 5:22, he makes the simple point that spiritual

---

[5] John Chrysostom, *An Address on Vainglory and The Right Way for Parents to Bring Up Their Children, Section 22. Translated by Max L. W. Laistner in Pagan Culture in the Later Roman Empire* (NY: Cornell University Press, 1951), 9.

[6] Ibid, section 28 (page 11); the section on the importance of teaching the Bible stories is found in section 39-47 (pages 13-16).

leadership in the home results in godly leadership in the Church: "If we administer our households in this way, then we will be fit for leadership of the church, for the household is a little church."[7] In another sermon, he urges husbands to teach the message of the assembly in the home. He exhorts, "let your household become a church. Do this in order that the devil may be banished and that evil demon – the enemy of our salvation – may run away. The grace of the Holy Spirit will rest there at once, and all peace and harmony will surround the residents."[8] Chrysostom's vision of the home as a "little church" speaks volumes. The home should be a place where the values, teachings, and reality of the body of Christ are lived out. When that occurs, like the church, the home will be a place of worship, instruction, and peace.

This evidence of religion in the home among the early church shows that some serious Christians in first few centuries continued the biblical mandate of passing along faith in the home and understood that the home is key. While the phrase "family worship" wasn't coined until much later, prominent writers in the early Church viewed family prayer, worship, and instruction as critical to the future of the Church.

---

[7] John Chrysostom, *Homilies on Ephesians* 20.I, 6, on Eph 5:22ff. Cited in Ferguson, *Inheriting Wisdom*, 11-12.
[8] John Chrysostom, *Homilies on Genesis* 2.4 [13], on Gen. 1:2. Cited in Ferguson, *Inheriting Wisdom*, 11-12.

The Medieval Church

As the church entered the Middle Ages, several developments led away from an emphasis on personal discipleship and parents training their own children. The rise of a professionalized and celibate priesthood, the growth of Christendom and its accompanying "dumbing down" of Christian commitment, the formation of monastic orders for the truly religious, and the general decline in literacy all conspired against making family worship a priority. Instead, instruction in faith and worship was centered at the Church building and conducted by formal Church leadership, which represented an increasingly smaller portion of the general population. Consequently, passing along faith in the home became extremely rare during the medieval period. Despite attempts to reform the Church in the Middle Ages, both from leadership and the laity, by the late medieval period, average Christians were not well-versed in a biblical worldview, let alone capable of teaching their children the essentials of the faith. In fact, during the sixteenth-century reformation, one thing that Catholic and Protestant leaders could agree upon was that the average person in Christian Europe was not genuinely Christian. Faith needed to be re-rooted all over again.[9]

---

[9] For this theme see Scott Hendrix, "Rerooting the Faith: The Reformation as Re-Christianization," *Church History* 69 (2000): 558-577.

The Protestant Reformation

The Protestant Reformation of the early sixteenth century sought to reform Christianity from the abuses and stifling traditions of the medieval era. This reform movement was characterized by a renewed focus on salvation by grace alone through faith, an emphasis on Christ, a rejection of burdensome traditions, and a return to Scripture as the primary authority in the Church. Erasmus of Rotterdam, the preeminent Christian scholar and cultural commentator whose work helped launch the Reformation, emphasized Christ-centered religion that downplayed ritual and form and advocated for personal and in-depth knowledge of the Bible by all Christians. His radical vision for a biblically literate laity whose personal piety went beyond that of church leaders runs throughout his writings, and his concern for getting the message of Christianity deep into the hearts of every person impacted the entire Reformation.

The mainline reformers, such as Martin Luther and John Calvin, sought to reform the Church by maintaining a connection with the state. Radicals like the Anabaptists sought to sever ties with government altogether, expressed dramatically by their rejection of infant baptism, which was critical to the state-church alliance. Despite the diversity of belief, all Protestants agreed that their reform initiatives must include renewed homes permeated by genuine faith, biblical literacy, prayer, and worship. One of the ways that the Reformers sought to train the average Christian was through systematic teaching booklets called "catechisms." In the patristic church, those receiving instruction in the faith before baptism were called "catechumens" (learners), and Protestants adapted that concept in their attempt to reform Christianity. Some booklets for instruction of Christians existed in the Middle Ages, but the Reformation's insistence on biblical literacy produced a flood of manuals of Christian instruction, or catechisms, in the sixteenth century.

The Anabaptist leader Balthasar Hubmaier was one of the first reformers to develop a guide for instructing people in evangelical faith, but Martin Luther's Small Catechism is the most famous and widely distributed guide. Published in 1529, it provides a tool for instructing members of the household in the faith, and that instruction is given in the home by fathers. Small Catechism has six sections that seek to ground the family in foundational teaching of biblical Christianity in a topical format. Each section states the topic, followed by the phrase "The simple way a father should present it to his household." The topic headings for the catechism are the Ten Commandments, Apostle's Creed, Lord's Prayer, Baptism, Confession, and Communion. Importantly, an appendix to the document provides a short guide for how a father can teach his family the faith at home through prayer and singing in the morning, evening, and at meals.[10]

---

[10] The smaller catechism is available in many English translations. For a convenient and modern translation see http://www.projectwittenberg.org/pub/resources/text/wittenberg/wittenberg-boc.html#sc.

Luther's insistence on the home as a place of worship and instruction is well-known and appears throughout his writings. One of his famous statements comes in a sermon on Abraham where Luther, like Chrysostom before him, likens the home to a church and school:

> Abraham had in his tent a house of God and a church, just as today any godly and pious head of a household instruct his children…in godliness. Therefore, such a house is actually a school and church, and the head of the household is a bishop and priest in his house.[11]

The critical role of the home and the head of the household for the advancement of evangelical faith could not be more plainly stated. In addition to straightforward instruction, Reformers also viewed singing as a powerful and effective way to establish the evangelical message in the mind and hearts of Christians. Luther made significant contributions to Christian hymnology with songs like "A Mighty Fortress is Our God," and he sought to encourage singing in the home as an effective way to proclaim the gospel. Reformers not only spread the gospel through preaching but also through singing in church and at home. Clearly, Luther understood that the home was essential for passing along the faith and he promoted family worship in evangelical congregations. Luther's contribution was important, but others

---

[11] Luther's Works, Vol. 4, *Lectures on Genesis*, pg. 384.

called even more vigorously for family worship as a priority – and obligation – of the Christian home.

John Calvin, the major Reformer of Geneva, influenced millions of Protestants through his ministry and writings and what we know as the Reformed tradition. Echoing Chrysostom's phrase, Calvin repeatedly refers to the home as a church where Christ was to be central and instruction in the Word a priority. Commenting on the conversion of an entire household in Acts 16, he writes,

> Anyone, who is included among the children of God, who is entrusted to exercise authority over others...is unworthy if he does not take care to give a place to Christ. Therefore, let each of the faithful strive to organize his household as an image of the church. All the godly ought to exert themselves to that every kind of superstition is prohibited in their homes. They are not to have godless families but retain them in the fear of the Lord.[12]

The emphasis placed on the home typifies the tradition that follows in Calvin's footsteps. The importance of family worship among sixteenth-century Reformers comes together in a formal capacity in The Westminster Confession of Faith (1647), a document that has had a profound effect on churches in the Reformed tradition.

---

[12] Cited in William J. Bouwsma, *John Calvin. A Sixteenth Century Portrait* (NY: Oxford University Press, 1988), 211-212.

Puritan leaders adopted this confession in England amidst a battle with the King of England over issues of religious freedom, democracy, and civil rights. This comprehensive guide for Reformed English faith specifically states that "God is to be worshipped everywhere in spirit and in truth; as in private families daily, and in secret each one by himself."[13]

That same year, Scottish Churches produced a short document, The Directory for Family Worship, which sought to encourage and guide worship in homes across their nation for the advancement of the Christian faith. In its words,

> ...it is expedient and necessary that secret worship of each person alone, and private worship of families, be pressed and set up; that, with national reformation, the profession and power of godliness, both personal and domestick [sic], be advanced.[14]

English Puritans and other Reformed Christians brought this conviction and practice of family worship with them to America. Many eighteenth-century Puritan leaders such as Richard Baxter, Jonathan Edwards, Matthew Henry, and others held up family worship as a

---

[13] *Westminster Confession of Faith*, Chapter 21 Section 6; http://www.pcaac.org/wp-content/uploads/2012/11/WCFScriptureProofs.pdf (Accessed March 19, 2018).

[14] http://www.reformed.org/documents/wcf_standards/index.html?mainframe=/documents/wcf_standards/p417-direct_fam_worship.html (Accessed March 19, 2018).

normal and essential part of Christian life.[15] An eloquent expression of this conviction comes from Samuel Davies, Puritan preacher and President of Princeton:

> If you love your children; if you would bring down the blessing of heaven upon your families: if you would have your children make their houses the receptacles of religion when they set up in life for themselves; if you would have religion survive in this place, and be conveyed from age to age; if you would deliver your own souls – I beseech, I entreat, I charge you to begin and continue the worship of God in your families from this day to the close of your lives…Consider family religion not merely as a duty imposed by authority, but as your greatest privilege granted by divine grace.[16]

Some in the Reformed tradition took this requirement so seriously that they refused communion to men who failed to practice regular family worship in their homes. While few would take such an extreme view today, it demonstrates how normal and expected family worship was in previous generations.

---

[15] For a survey of American Puritans and their emphasis on family worship, see Donald S. Whitney, *Family Worship* (Wheaton, IL: Crossway, 2016), 33-38.

[16] Cited in Whitney, *Family Worship*, 36.

The Early Restoration Movement

The American Restoration Movement, led by Thomas and Alexander Campbell, Barton Stone, and Walter Scott, was born at the beginning of the nineteenth century and was greatly impacted by the Reformed tradition of worship and piety. Multiple sources attest to the importance of family worship in the culture of the restoration leaders. The Campbells came from a Presbyterian environment and inherited the practice of family worship as a normal part of their home life. Alexander Campbell, the unquestioned thought leader of the early Restoration Movement, was an ardent proponent and practitioner of regular family worship. Robert Richardson, Campbell's close friend and biographer, describes family worship as a regular feature of the Campbell household. He writes,

> It was the evening that was always specially devoted to social and religious improvement. At an early hour the entire household, domestics included, assembled in the spacious parlor, each one having hymns or some Scripture lessons to recite. After these were heard, often with pertinent and encouraging remarks from Mr. Campbell, the Scriptures were read in regular sequence, with questions to those present as to the previous connection or the scope of the chapter. These being briefly considered, he would call upon Mrs. Campbell [Selina], who had a good voice, to lead in singing a psalm or

spiritual song, in which he himself would heartily join, and then kneeling down would most reverently and earnestly present before the throne of grace their united thanksgivings and petitions for divine guardianship and guidance.[17]

Richardson goes on to observe that Campbell was no mere formalist when it came to religion in the home but worked to make sure that family worship didn't become stale or dull. He continues:

Such was the customary order, but the details were often varied to suit the occasion. Family worship was not allowed to become a mere routine. He knew well how to maintain its interest, by making it a means of real instruction and enjoyment; and by encouraging familiar inquiry on the part of the young, he managed to bring forward and to impress indelibly the most charming practical lessons from the sacred writing, having always something novel and agreeable to impart zest and interest to exercises which in many cases are apt to become monotonous by frequent repetition. In these praiseworthy endeavors to bring up children in the nurture of the Lord, much was due also to the judicious arrangements and hearty co-operation of Mrs. Campbell, who like her predeces-

---

[17] Robert Richardson, *The Memoirs of Alexander Campbell*, Vol II (Philadelphia: J.B. Lippincott & Co., 1870), 300-301.

sor, made all things subservient to the desired end, and in her husband's absence herself officiated at the family altar when there happened to be no brother present accustomed to the duty.[18]

Selina Campbell's recollections echo those of Richardson; she emphasized the way that her late-husband's personal love of God and his family were revealed at the "family circle." In her words,

All of its members were lovingly assembled, morning and evening, to unite in worshipping God the Father, through his beloved Son, through and by the Holy Spirit. Nothing was permitted to interrupt the regularity of this sublime privilege. It was not attended to as a cold, formal duty, but it was made inspiring to all in attendance, by wife and children taking part, either in reading, verses, turn about, in the precious book, or reciting passages of Scripture. Hymns were often recited, and sometimes chapters and part of chapters. Servants were all called to be present; singing with spirit and understanding, accompanied the family devotional exercises.[19]

---

[18] Ibid, 301.
[19] Selina Campbell, *Home Life and Reminiscence of Alexander Campbell* (St Louis, MO: Burns Publishing, 1882), 18-19.

At the height of his influence as president of Bethany College in 1850, Alexander Campbell published a treatise entitled Family Culture, or Conversation in the Domestic Circle at the Carlton House. This fascinating and sophisticated booklet shows families how to conduct Christian instruction in the home, utilizing a dialogue form similar, but not identical, to traditional catechisms. In the preface, Campbell doesn't mince words about the importance of explicit household worship but offers a rousing call to heartfelt and authentic worship in the home. Building on the meaning of the word Bethel (house of God), he writes:

> All Christian dwellings should be Bethels – houses consecrated to God, in which his word should be read, his praises sung, and his name invoked on all the days of the year…Are not Christian householders as much bound by divine authority to bring up their families for the Lord – to nurture and train them for the royal family of heaven! And what son of God is there who has a heart, a tongue, and a Bible – children and servants under his care, and will not anoint his pillar, erect his altar, and worship the Lord constantly in his family? Thus teaching his children by his example how much he loves and delights in God, and with what pure affec-

tion and tender love he seeks their moral excellence and the eternal life.[20]

Campbell's influence was felt throughout the Restoration Movement as thousands of visitors, students, colleagues, and friends joined him for worship in his home. The practice among the Campbells impacted later leaders such as J.W. McGarvey and Moses Lard, men who, after his death, approvingly recalled Campbell's attention to family worship and their participation in it at Bethany.[21] The Campbell emphasis on daily devotion to God in the home was not just a family quirk but a practice embraced by others in the movement. Barton Stone's Christian Messenger includes exhortations to family worship; it also calls out those who neglect family worship for their failures as Christian parents.[22]

Family worship was also a well-known part of the daily life and mentoring of Walter Scott, the most successful evangelist among the early restoration preachers. Scott's personal piety and commitment to family worship matched that of Campbell. Regarding the raising of children, Scott commented, "Parents may be divided into three sorts: animal parents, rational parents,

---

[20] Alexander Campbell, *Family Culture; or, Conversations in the Domestic Circle at the Carlton House* (London: Hall & Company, 1850), 16-17.

[21] See M.W. McGarvey, *The Autobiography of J.W. McGarvey* (Lexington, KY: College of the Bible, 1960), 16; also, Moses Lard, "Alexander Campbell," *Lard's Quarterly* (April 1866): 265.

[22] For an example from the Stone sphere of influence, see "Family Prayer," *Christian Messenger* 4 (1830): 189-190.

and religious parents." Scott believed that Christian parents must combine all three "sorts," attending to the spiritual needs of children as well as their physical and intellectual ones. He was particularly known for using family worship in his home as a way to mentor young ministers. In the Scott home, family worship occurred in the mornings and included recitation of memorized Scripture by every member of the household (including guests), singing of hymns, explanation of Bible passages, and prayers. The practice of incorporating ministry students into his own family's worship made a life-long impact on these preachers.[23] The big four of the Restoration movement (Thomas and Alexander Campbell, Barton Stone, and Walter Scott) believed in the importance of family worship and the practice of it continued on into the late nineteenth century.[24]

Throughout Christian history, the home has been viewed as a critical and paramount place for passing along faith to the next generation. Beyond the practical value for ensuring multigenerational faithfulness, exalting God in worship and praise in the home has been rightfully understood as a duty and a God-exalting practice. While it has not always born the title "family worship," the practice of regular training in the faith and focus on God in the home is a consistent feature of

---

[23] Dwight E. Stevenson, *Walter Scott: Voice of the Golden Oracle. A Biography* (Joplin, MO: College Press, 1946), 137-143.

[24] Family worship was even a daily feature in the home of David Lipscomb, the influential long-time editor of the *Gospel Advocate*. See Robert E. Hooper, *Crying in the Wilderness. A Biography of David Lipscomb* (Nashville: David Lipscomb College, 1979), 176.

faithful Christians in the past. Interestingly, family worship seems to shine most brightly during times of revival, reformation, and restoration, when biblical Christianity is flourishing. The call to family worship is both biblically sound and historically grounded. When Christians take this call seriously, the results in the lives of children and their churches are amazing, and God is glorified.

The Effectiveness of Family Worship

Family worship has biblical and historical foundations, but it also is extremely effective for ensuring multi-generational faithfulness. Parents must answer the call to family worship and assume God's role for the spiritual instruction of their children because they are the most effective teachers their children will ever have. This is not because they are necessarily gifted and creative and highly educated in biblical studies. Rather, it's because parents have the most time with their children and a deep personal bond with them. Children naturally love, respect, and look up to their parents. This is especially true in the younger years, before they naturally begin to assert their independence during adolescence.

When parents actively impart faith to their children, it is likely to stick for life. Parents are physically with their children more than anyone else. If they take opportunities through daily rhythms to teach their children, it will be extremely effective. A week of church camp can help a young person's faith, but it won't counteract the fifty-one weeks of secular messaging he or she receives at school, through media, and from friends. A weekly Sunday school class can be helpful for learning the Bible, but it's simply not enough time or material to counter six days a week of secular influences. Parents who teach their children at home on a regular basis take advantage of precious time to shape and mold their children in the Christian message while they are still developing their worldview. The key, of course, is taking the time. Implementing a regular practice of family worship creates time and space for spiritual instruction.

Consistent family worship effectively communicates faithfulness to children while also speaking volumes into their hearts about what Christianity is all about. Family worship demonstrates the comprehensive nature of Christian discipleship. If children only worship God and receive instruction in the faith at the assembly of the Church once or twice a week, they may see faith as something saved for certain religious settings. This, however, is not what biblical Christianity and discipleship look like. Christians are called to take up our cross and follow Jesus daily and in every sphere of life. Too many Christians act, talk, and think one way at Church and a completely different way at home, school, work, or play. Family worship helps break down this false separation by showing that our faith is at the center of life.

One of the great lessons that children need to learn is what things in life are most important. Parents who embrace the call to family worship communicate loudly and clearly to their children the priority of their home. We can say that Christ is the Lord of our life, but our kids will see how much attention we give Him in our homes. Many Christians, overwhelmed by the busyness of modern life, think they don't have time for family worship. But if we are honest, we must admit that we do have time. The problem is that we spend too much time on things that are not eternally important or that actually harm our children's spiritual lives. By making time for family worship, we are sending a powerful message to children about God's central place in our family. When we turn off the TV, power off the devices, or put away the board game to focus on worshiping God, we are making a powerful testimony about the Lordship of Christ in our home. When our children see our words put into action, they will grasp the message and embrace that faith for themselves and their families.

Conclusion

The call to family worship is based on a firm biblical foundation, proven historical precedent, and its effectiveness for passing along faith to the next generation. However, regular family worship is not a silver bullet that will solve all family problems and provide absolute guarantees of multi-generational faithfulness, nor is it the only practice that will shape our children's faith. Acts of service to neighbors and brothers and sisters in Christ, ethical living, private devotion, participation in church education programs, Christian education, and worship in the assembly of the Church all have important roles to play in faith development. The point here is simply that parents must once again regain their rightful place as the principal shapers of their children's faith and family worship is a time-tested and biblically sound practice that enables parents to obey God's call to disciple their children.

The Blessing of Family Worship

Family worship will help parents fulfill their calling to raise children in the Lord, which is a duty and obligation inherent in Christian parenting. I want to stress, however, that regular home-based worship will also bring many, many blessings to your family. One day, a minister friend of mine and I were talking about the need for more families to seek the Lord together in the home, and he became overwhelmed with emotion as he shared what it had done in his family's life. Anything that we do that it is in accordance with God's will and nature will bring blessings, and family worship is no exception. Some blessings are obvious and yield immediate fruit in the life of your family. You will likely see them right before your eyes after only a few months. Others, on the other hand, will only be evident as the years go by and your children grow into adults. A regular practice of family worship will produce six major blessings in your family: It will unify your family, provide space for family dialogue, become a life-giving spiritual tradition, reveal weaknesses in the family unit, invigorate Christian marriages, and provide training ground for worship in the assembly.

1. **It will unify your family**. One of the most obvious blessings of family worship is that your family will draw closer together. A reality of our modern world is that families are fragmented and pulled in different directions by the seemingly endless number of activities our kids (and parents) can choose to be involved in. Most of these things are not inherently bad. In fact, they have some value in instilling discipline, teamwork, fair-play, physical health, and musical talent into the life of your child. Having said that, the tyranny of over-busyness must be recognized and guarded against in order to experience the blessing of family worship. Christian parents who make a commitment to regular worship in the home will find themselves saying no to more activities, so they can have this important time together as a family. Imagine a family that has developed a regular pattern of gathering without cell phones, television, or devices of any kind – just the family together for the purpose of worshiping God. Having an oasis of time together itself will help your family connect in powerful ways. When the spiritual component of worship is added, a unity develops that is based on the deepest of all connections, a oneness in the Lordship of Christ. Praying together is a particularly powerful way to draw closer as a family. If you've participated in a long-term prayer group

that meets regularly, you know the intimacy and connectedness that develop through prayer. It's part of the way God designed human relationships. When we speak to our Creator with another person who shares the image of God and is also humbly seeking the will of God, a unique relationship forms. For families, this means that part of your prayer together should be to intercede specifically for members of your nuclear family. I love to hear my kids praying for one another about upcoming tests, troubles with their pets, or other small things that concern children. It gives me a window into their concerns and hearts, and they in turn are developing hearts for one another.

2. **It will provide space for family dialogue**. On a more basic but still important level, family worship provides space for open family dialogue, where mundane things that affect everyone can be discussed. Before or after the official worship part, we often find ourselves figuring out schedules for the next day or week. This part of family worship functions like announcements in the larger church setting. Activities and events are coming up that we all need to know about, and people in our lives have things going on that we need to process as a family and pray about. As kids get older and have more freedom, this component of that time together has been increasingly important. Having a regular place for

your family to talk about God, life, friends, morals, Christian teaching, and scheduling issues will naturally bring your family together. An old saying captures the point: "A family that prays together, stays together." Again, while family worship is not a silver bullet that will solve all your family's difficulties, one of its blessings is that it helps keep your family unified.

3. **It will become a life-giving spiritual tradition**. Another blessing of family worship is that you will be creating a tradition that will be passed to your grandchildren and great-grandchildren. The classic movie Fiddler on the Roof has many famous songs, but one of the favorites is "Tradition" for the ways it expresses the positive and life-giving nature of communal practices handed down to subsequent generations. To be sure, tradition can become stifling, legalistic, and mindless, but every culture and community has healthy traditions that give them a sense of identity and helps keep them oriented to the world around them. Can you imagine how difficult and time-consuming it would be as a culture to create new processes all the time for the activities we engage in? Traditions are an essential part of human community. Some towns pride themselves on their traditions, whether it is having a Turkey Trot every year or a Groundhog Day celebration to anticipate the end of winter. A

family unit is a community, and families thrive when they have healthy traditions and routines that bring stability to the community over a long period of time and create memories that are shared across the generations. On top of that, kids love family traditions, whether it's about how and when to open Christmas presents, what we do on birthdays, or where we go camping every year. A tradition that developed in our family was that I would take one or more of my kids to the store to pick out donuts for breakfast on Saturday mornings. This tradition lasted for years until we got a little more health conscious, but even now, it's still tradition that we have something different for breakfast on Saturdays, and Daddy is in charge. I'll never forget the year that my oldest daughter was graduating from high school and I nearly (nearly, I say) broke out into tears at the grocery store picking out donuts, realizing that she wouldn't be around anymore to get donuts with me. Traditions hold generations together, and they can often develop into an emotional attachment that goes beyond rationality. Now, think about your family's traditions, the things you do because that's who you are. There's a good chance that when your children grow up and leave home, they will take at least some of those traditions into their own marriages and families. Here's the point: Children who grow up with the tradition of regular family worship will likely continue that practice in their homes with their children. It's what you do. The blessings they experience in family worship will be something they want their children to experience as well. Family worship will be one of those good, multi-generational traditions. Your decision to commit to regular family worship will yield spiritual blessings and dividends far beyond your own family, but also into the lives of your grandchildren and their children. By faith and hope, I'm looking forward to years from now, when my grown children with their own families gather at our house for holidays and have family worship together. It's what our family does.

4. **It will reveal weaknesses in the family unit**. Ironically, another blessing of family worship is that it will reveal weaknesses in your family. On the surface, this may seem like a negative thing, but there can be no growth if we aren't aware of things in our lives that need to be addressed. Ideally, family worship will be a place where the family gathers to worship God but also to discuss things happening at school, church, and other spheres of life. Having this regular place to talk is valuable, especially as children reach adolescence and need a safe place to ask questions about life, faith, and family. A spirit of openness and simply having a time set aside for discussion will bring out things that may need to be addressed. Worship and prayer are difficult to

fake, and a hesitant spirit or scowling face can often help us know that something is wrong with one or more of our children. It may be a problem they are having in their social lives, or it might be a problem with mom and dad that is exposed during family worship. Sometimes, when we gather for worship, it becomes a place where God exposes difficulties and sin that needs to be addressed. If parents are rushing family worship so they can start their favorite TV show or other worldly activity, it can serve as a wake-up call to our spiritual priorities. If we are truly worshiping God, everyone, including parents, will be convicted and taught and shaped into the image of Christ. Part of that is having our weaknesses revealed so they can be healed.

5. **It will invigorate Christian marriages**. Another great blessing of family worship is that it has the potential to invigorate marriages. By its very nature, it brings husbands and wives together for a common purpose that is at the heart of God's will for the family, and that practice will naturally strengthen the husband and wife relationship. Sometimes, Christian husbands and wives can fall victim to the "silo effect" in their spiritual relationship. Both are godly and good disciples of Christ, but their spiritual growth rarely occurs together in a common spiritual activity; the husband follows his spiritual routine with a Bible reading plan or a group of friends that he

prays with, while the wife similarly has her favorite radio program or Bible study that she is doing, but the two of them may struggle to pray together and interact with God's Word. The spiritual oneness that God designed for marriage is often stunted by the husband and wife failing to spend time together in Scripture and prayer. But a couple that commits to regular family worship with their children will see that spiritual exercise spilling over into their relationship with one another. And who says family worship is only for families with kids old enough to participate? Our family was inspired to family worship in part by the godly example of an elderly couple who put us up for the night while we were on a road trip with our three young children. After dinner, they invited us to join them for their evening tradition of Bible reading and prayer. They were in the habit of worshiping God together, just the two of them, and they gave us a vision of couples growing together in Christ into their later years.

I believe that most Christian women want their husbands to lead the family spiritually. For a variety of reasons, however, Christian husbands often struggle to provide the spiritual leadership that comes with being the head of the home. A man who commits to leading his family in worship – and who follows through with it – will find himself more respected by his wife and more in tune with her needs, wants, and desires, which will result in a stronger marriage.

6. **It will provide training ground for worship in the assembly of the church**. When our children were very young, we spent a lot of time in family worship working on how to be still, pray, and listen to Scripture as it is read. Those early years paid dividends when we arrived on Sunday to worship with the rest of the church. Children who experience regular family worship know how to behave in the assembly because they have had a lot of practice in the home. They recognize and understand the rhythms of prayer and singing, and they can listen carefully to the proclamation of the Word. Please don't misunderstand me as saying family worship is just practice for the "real thing" on Sunday morning – that simply isn't true. However, an obvious blessing of worshiping together at home is that it will positively affect your worship with the broader church.

Getting Started with Family Worship

Many parents love the idea of family worship and may even see the blessings that it would bring to their family's life, but they don't have any practical experience and don't know how to get started. If you feel this way, you aren't alone. That's what this guide is all about. Before continuing, I want to give you five pieces of advice for getting started with family worship.

First, family worship must come from conviction. Through prayer and reflection, you must become convinced and convicted that this is something you need to do for your family, for yourselves, and for the honor of God. Feel the conviction that Joshua experienced when he declared, "As for me and my house, we will serve the Lord" (Joshua 24:15). Satan will surely try to discourage you and keep you from your commitment. If you feel like family worship is an extra-curricular spiritual activity rather than an essential Christian practice, you probably won't last very long. But if it's born of conviction, you will implement strategies that make it a regular part of your family's life.

Second, family worship begins with fathers. In my view, it's the father's responsibility to make sure family worship happens. As noted above, Paul singled out fathers as responsible for spiritual instruction because – as the Christ-like servant leader of the family – he is ultimately accountable for his family's spiritual welfare. For many dads, this is a daunting idea made more difficult by the fact that most men have no model for conducting family worship. That's one reason I've put this guide together—to help dads carry out God's calling for them. If you need help, I encourage you to ask your minister or another man in your church known for leading his family in worship. The main thing is that you step up and prayerfully commit to the challenge. For some wives, the idea of the husband leading family worship is hard to imagine. Be prayerful, understanding, and encouraging as the topic of family worship is broached with him. If your husband is not a believer, take Timothy's mother as your model and raise up a child in the faith without the father's involvement (II Timothy 1:5; Acts 16:1). Mom and dad working together is the biblical ideal, but if one parent will not participate, it should not keep the rest from family worship.

Third, family worship must be a scheduled priority. In the modern world, family schedules are increasingly fragmented and over-booked. As one mom told me, "If it's not on the schedule it's not happening." In the same way, it's important to schedule family worship. Sit down as a family and figure out when and where family worship will take place. Make sure everyone knows about it. More than likely, it will require sacrificing lesser things for something greater. That means saying no to some activities that compete with the family's time together in worship. It really is that simple. For many families, the best time, especially when kids are younger, is right before bedtime. For others, it may need to be at dinner time or even in the early morning.

As you develop a schedule, consider the following:

1. Be consistent but realistic. On late nights or when traveling, you might shorten it to a song and prayer, or even just a prayer. The point is that the family has paused to focus on God together, even if just for a few minutes.

2. Adjust the schedule as needed. If you are struggling to worship together every day, consider start-

ing with two nights per week and work up to the six-night routine.

3. Include guests. Don't let the presence of out of town friends or evening guests keep you from family worship. Invite them to join you. You may inspire them to similar practices in their home, just as our friends inspired us.

Fourth, it's never too late to start. You may be thinking, "My kids are all grown and it's too late to start family worship" or "my kids are already in High School, and they just won't do it." These are lies that Satan will use to discourage you from starting family worship. It's never too late to start. It still honors God to worship Him at home, even if it's just husband and wife sitting in an empty nest. Plus, you can share your newfound experience of family worship with your grown kids when they come home for visits and encourage them to start this tradition in their homes. As for the high school kids, there may be initial opposition, but there is also a great chance that one or more of your children will love it and really enjoy focused time with mom and dad while navigating the travails of the teenage years. Keep in mind the goal of honoring God in the home and receiving instruction in the Christian faith. These always need to happen, regardless of your life situation.

Fifth, be accountable for your commitment. We all have weaknesses and often give up on the promises we have made, especially when it gets hard. Accountability is the universally recognized support to keeping commitments, whether it's weight loss program, avoiding bad habits, or other personal goals. After you have made the decision for family worship, tell another family about your plan and give them permission to ask you how it's going. Ask them to encourage you if you begin to slack off. Talk to your minister about this vow and ask him to pray for you and keep you accountable. Better yet, talk to your kids about this commitment and let them know that you are making family worship a new feature in your home. More than likely, younger children will love this time together and eagerly remind you if you begin to falter.

The Heart of Family Worship

Simplicity is one important key to successful and consistent family worship. This guide is organized around four simple components that are essential to family worship: **Read the Word, Recite Truth, Sing to the Lord, & Pray Always**. This chapter describes what should happen during each of these elements of worship and provides tips for success.

Read the Word

But as for you, continue in what you have learned and have firmly believed, knowing from whom you learned it and how from childhood you have been acquainted with the sacred writings, which are able to make you wise for salvation through faith in Christ Jesus. All Scripture is breathed out by God and profitable for teaching, for reproof, for correction, and for training in righteousness, that the man of God may be complete, equipped for every good work.

II Timothy 3:14-17

The most basic element of family worship is reading Holy Scripture together, something directly linked to our conviction that Scripture is the inspired Word of God that changes the heart and transforms the mind. Every time you gather for family worship, you should read the Bible. The suggested Bible reading guides in Chapter Four can help your family consistently read portions of Scripture throughout the year.

One of the most important principles to keep in mind when planning for reading the Bible together is "**structured flexibility**." On one hand, it's essential to have a plan so that each time you gather you have a predetermined set of Scripture to read. Deciding each night which passage to read will not yield good results. Take some time to think about what plan will work best for your family and then follow it. On the other hand, it's also vital to be flexible and adjust as needed. Sometimes, you may have to make changes, such as when it becomes clear that you bit off more than you can chew, your church adopts a congregation-wide reading plan, or when you sense that some other material would be good for your family during a particularly challenging season of life. Have a plan and be willing to adjust it as necessary.

Another thing to keep in mind is factoring in time for Bible discussion. Discussion prompts are provided in

Chapter Four as ideas to get your family thinking and talking about the Bible. Sometimes the point of a passage will be simple; other times, it may be profound. Children often have lots of questions, and that is the way it should be. If you don't have the answers, write the questions down and spend some time thinking, studying, and asking a minister or other spiritual leader to help. Come back later with a reasoned answer for your family. This will demonstrate to your children a humble and diligent attitude toward Scripture.

Tips for reading the Bible together

I've included some tips and tricks for reading the Bible as a family. These can be mixed and matched. Try different things and see what works for your family.

1. Retell the passage. One way to work through a Bible passage is to have someone retell the message to the rest of the family. In the narrative sections, this can be a lot of fun and great for children, especially if the story is acted out or retold dramatically.

2. Bible discussion. Every night there should be some discussion of the Bible. A couple of nights a week, I encourage you to have an extended discussion of the Bible passage you read that night. Page two of the Quarterly Reading Schedule provides some questions designed to help you discuss and apply the Bible reading for the night.

3. Bible quizzes. Young children especially like to be quizzed over the reading material. Saying, "there will be a quiz after we read the text" helps kids focus. True/false and multiple-choice questions can be made up on the spot by dad or mom and are a lot of fun.

4. Listen to the Bible. Try listening to the text of Scripture. You can purchase CDs or digital files that include readings of the Scriptures. Or, go to online resources like www.biblegateway.com for a free audio version of the Bible in multiple translations. If you are using a device, be careful that it doesn't become a distraction.

5. Designated readers. You might try making each night of the week a different person's night to read. For example: Monday is Joey's night, Tuesday is Bailey's night, etc. This gives kids a sense of importance and belonging in the structure.

6. Read around the room. Reading a verse or two at a time around the room is a classic way to keep everyone involved and participating. As children grow in their ability to read, encourage them to read the passage of Scripture.

7. Use a good translation. Use a standard translation and make sure everyone has the same one. Using the same translation helps everyone stay on the same page. My family uses the English Standard Version for its readability and accuracy.

8. Bring your Bibles. It's very important that everyone has a copy of the Scriptures during family worship. Not only is it a good habit to develop, but it also greatly helps the discussion portion of the Bible reading. There may be times when it's appropriate to just listen to Scripture, but it's generally helpful to follow along.

9. Read during meals. One way to ensure that you read the text every day is to have one person read at the beginning of a meal. This is an old tradition in Christian history and can result in interesting and spiritual discussions breaking out during mealtime.

10. Pray for understanding. Develop a habit of uttering a simple prayer before each Bible reading that asks God to bless the reading of His Word. It could be the same prayer each time, or something different that expresses the same idea. *"Lord, help us to understand your Word as we read it now."* It helps prepare the heart and mind for the Word and promotes a prayerful posture toward Scripture.

Recite Truth

How can a young man keep his way pure? By guarding it according to your word. With my whole heart I seek you; let me not wander from your commandments! I have stored up your word in my heart, that I might not sin against you.

Blessed are you, O LORD; teach me your statutes! With my lips I declare all the rules[a] of your mouth. In the way of your testimonies I delight as much as in all riches. I will meditate on your precepts and fix my eyes on your ways. I will delight in your statutes; I will not forget your word.

Psalm 119:9-16

This classic Psalm emphasizes the importance of meditating on God's Word and having it on the lips. For this reason, reciting truth – mainly the words of Scripture – should become a standard part of each gathering for family worship. "Being transformed by the renewal of the mind" (Romans 12:1) involves repeating words of truth and memorizing key words from God that will eventually become part of your mind, heart, and vocabulary. Memorizing foundational truths is especially important for children because their minds are so malleable and they can absorb lengthy passages. Children memorize easily – make the most of that time! In this guide, each day recommends a different foundational passage to recite as a family. These passages are: The Ten Commandments (Exodus 20), the Ancient Confession, the Lord's Prayer (Matthew 6), Aaron's Blessing (Numbers 6), The Christ Hymn (Philippians 2), and Psalm 1. Later in this chapter, I've included these passages and an explanation of the historical and theological value of each one.

Tips for Memorization

In pre-modern times, memorization of important texts such as poetry, prose, and Scripture was basic to education and the transmission of knowledge from one generation to the next. With the information explosion, memorization has become less and less part of the modern educational system. Yet, memorization of Scripture is foundational for meditation and reflection, as well as for prayer and worship. We need to be people who can slow down and meditate on truth, and reciting it together as a family is an important step in that direction. Below are a few tips on memorizing and reciting Scripture in family worship.

1. Sing. One of the best ways to memorize is to put Scripture to song. Many people learned the books of the Bible by putting it to song, and the current revival of classical Christian education is recovering song as essential to learning in the early years.

2. Set goals. Commit as a family to memorizing the passages in this guide in a reasonable amount of time. Try memorizing the shorter selections first and then memorizing the others until you complete all of them. There's a lot of satisfaction in reciting these passages together as a family.

3. Rewards. Young children are especially motivated by rewards. A special trip to the ice cream café after memorizing one of the passages can be motivating. When our kids were younger and we had a fish tank, they could earn fish by reciting Scripture. Be creative and figure out what works for your family!

4. Chant. Chanting the passage together as a family will help you memorize it. This method is time tested and great for families. It might sound strange at first, but you'll get used to it, and the rhythm will drill the words into your mind.

5. Repetition. Repeat phrases and lines three times before moving on to something else. You can also do this as a call and response: The leader can say a phrase, and the family repeat it together (preferably three times), going line-by-line throughout the passage. The phrases being repeated can vary in length depending on your family and your familiarity with the passage. For example:

Leader: "Blessed is the man."

Family: "Blessed is the man, blessed is the man, blessed is the man."

6. Divide and conquer. Divide longer passages into smaller portions that can be tackled more quickly.

7. Accountability. Partner with another family to reach a memorization goal. Challenge that family to memorize certain sections by a certain date. The goal is not to "beat them" but to form a partnership designed to push both families forward in God's Word. You could also set goals with a small group or Bible class group.

8. Pray about your memorization. God delights in our desire to memorize His Word and the eternal truths it contains. Pray together about your memorization goals.

9. Long-term retention. Remember, the goal is long-term retention for future recall and the shaping of your family's worldview. Once a passage has been memorized, reciting it once a week in family worship will help keep it in your memory. Decades from now, your family will have a common body of material you can recite together.

10. Flash cards. Flash cards are great memorization tools. Be sure to memorize the Scripture reference as well as the text: "For God so loved the world...everlasting life." John 3:16

Six Foundational Passages to Memorize

The Ten Commandments

1. I am the Lord your God, who brought you out of Egypt, out of the land of slavery. You shall have no other gods before me.

2. You shall not make for yourself an idol in the form of anything in heaven above or on the earth beneath or in the waters below. You shall not bow down to them or worship them.

3. You shall not misuse the name of the Lord your God, for the Lord will not hold anyone guiltless who misuses his name.

4. Remember the Sabbath day by keeping it holy. Six days you shall labor and do all your work, but the seventh day is a sabbath to the Lord your God.

5. Honor your father and your mother, so that you may live long in the land the Lord your God is giving you.

6. You shall not murder.

7. You shall not commit adultery.

8. You shall not steal.

9. You shall not bear false testimony against your neighbor.

10. You shall not covet anything that belongs to your neighbor.

(NIV, 1984)

Historical and Theological Significance

When God led the children of Israel out of Egypt, He revealed Himself as a great deliverer and redeemer. He heard the cry of His people who were being oppressed. To enhance His relationship with them and confirm their special status as His people, God summoned Moses to Mount Sinai, where He spoke with him as "one man speaks to another." Out of this mountain-top meeting came the Ten Commandments, also known as the Decalogue. The Ten Commandments are foundational to Israel's covenant relationship with God and outline the major tenets of the Law of Moses.

The Ten Commandments have two tables. The first table includes the first four commands, which teach us how to relate to God and how to live in His presence. The second table includes the final six commands, which teach us to relate to one another in a way that pleases God and promotes communal peace. When Jesus was asked which is the greatest commandment in the law, (Matt 22:34-40) Jesus pointed to the essence of the Decalogue: Love the Lord Your God with all your heart, soul, mind, and strength (table 1) and love your neighbor as yourself (table 2). While the Ten Commandments have a lot of practical implications, they also contain deep spiritual insights that are beneficial for meditation.

The Ten Commandments are reaffirmed in the new covenant and remain important to our relationship with God. Although the Lord's Day became the special day of worship after Christ's resurrection, the fourth commandment continues to be relevant because it teaches us the importance of rest and devoting ourselves wholly to God. In a spiritual sense, the fourth commandment remains important because it reminds us that we must rest from our working to obtain salvation, knowing that Christ alone has achieved for us the salvation we could not gain on our own (Heb. 4:9). While no one is saved by perfect obedience to the Law of Moses, the Ten Commandments is a short and concise statement of eternal truths that form the basis of Christian ethical living. The Ten Commandments is found in Exodus 20:1-17 and Deuteronomy 5:6-21. The excerpt above is an adaptation and abbreviation of Exodus 20:1-17 (NIV, 1984). Be sure to memorize the Ten Commandments in numerical order and by saying the command. (1. I am the Lord your God...2. You shall not make...3. You shall not...)

By memorizing this together, your family joins the long-established custom in Christian History that instruction in the faith includes knowledge of the Ten Commandments.

The Ancient Confession

I believe in God the Father Almighty, the Creator of Heaven and Earth,

And in Jesus Christ, his only son, our Lord,

Who was conceived of the Holy Spirit, born of the Virgin Mary, suffered under Pontius Pilate, was crucified, died, and was buried.

The third day, He arose again from the dead. He ascended into heaven and sits at the right hand of God the Father Almighty, whence He shall come to judge the living and the dead.

I believe in the Holy Spirit, the Holy universal Church, the communion of saints, the forgiveness of sin, the resurrection of the body, and in life everlasting. Amen.

Historical and Theological Significance

The early Christian community held firmly to doctrines that set it apart from the surrounding pagan world. From the beginning Christians adhered to the Old Testament as inspired and authoritative Scripture, but they also devoted themselves to the Apostles' teachings. Within decades after the Apostles' deaths, many of these writings were collected into what came to be called the New Testament. Even as early as the late first century, Christians also began to formulate the essence of their faith in short hymns and summary statements that they could easily memorize and recite. While Christians did not view these summaries as authoritative in the same sense as Scripture, they were viewed as helpful, succinct statements of essential Christian teaching.

Several documents circulated in the second and third centuries that contained written expressions of what early Christian writers called the "rule of faith." The most common expression of it became known by the seventh century as the Apostles' Creed because it captured the beliefs of the Apostles. It may have originated as something confessed by new converts immediately prior to baptism. The text used above is an adaptation of the Old Roman Symbol, an earlier and shorter version of the later and more well-known Apostles' Creed. I've included this version because of its simplicity and antiquity. While the Ancient Confession is not a verbatim quote from Scripture, each of its tenets *is* explicitly expressed in the New Testament. It captures the essence of the rule of faith and is a valuable tool for helping retain and strengthen your grasp of the core of the Christian faith.

The Stone-Campbell movement was born at a time when creeds and confessions were misused to draw unwarranted boundaries between believers with little or no reference to the straightforward meaning of Scripture. For that reason, Stone-Campbell movement leaders often took a very low view of creeds. As these leaders lived in a time when adherence to detailed creeds fractured the unity of the Church, we can appreciate that non-credal impulse. At this time in our history, however, when our children are regularly attacked by secularism, materialism, liberalism, and religious pluralism, equipping them with an accessible and meaningful summary of the Christian worldview is essential. Many, like myself, have come to see the value of this Ancient Confession for its concise outline of the faith and broad picture of the heart of New Testament Christianity.[1] I strongly recommend memorizing it and reciting it together as a family.

The Lord's Prayer

Our Father in heaven, hallowed be your name.

Your kingdom come,
 your will be done, on earth as it is in heaven.
Give us this day our daily bread,
and forgive us our debts,
    as we also have forgiven our debtors.
And lead us not into temptation,
    but deliver us from evil.

For yours is the kingdom, and the power,

---

[1] See Everett Ferguson, *The Rule of Faith: A Guide* (Eugene, Oregon: Cascade Books, 2016), 83-90 for a good explanation of the value of the Rule of Faith for Christians today.

and the glory, forever.

Amen

Matthew 6:9-13

Historical and Theological Significance

The Lord's Prayer, also known as the model prayer, is Jesus Christ's direct teaching on how to pray. It expresses all the great themes that his followers should dwell upon in prayer: God's fatherhood and holiness; His reign as the king of kings; the hope and longing for His will to be done; His amazing care for our human physical needs and our spiritual need for forgiveness; our need to forgive others as we have been forgiven and the spiritual battle that rages in the heavenly realms and impacts our daily lives. Since Jesus warned against meaningless repetition in prayer, He did not intend the Lord's Prayer to be the only prayer we say. Instead, He simply provided a model that incorporates the essential elements of prayer. The Lord's Prayer represents fundamental phrases that should launch us into expanded and personalized expressions of love, devotion, and petition.

Committing the Lord's Prayer to memory is key for your spiritual growth and development. Historically, it also provides a powerful common prayer that can be said together as a family and as a community of faith.

Millions of believers around the world can quote this prayer together, which is a powerful testimony to Christian unity. The version cited above is from Matthew 6:9-13. The final phrase ("For yours is the kingdom...") is found in some manuscripts but included in the footnote of the ESV. I include it above because it likely represents an ancient rendition and provides a lyrical conclusion to the prayer that is well-known in the English-speaking world through the King James Version.

Aaron's Blessing

The Lord bless you and keep you;

the Lord make his face to shine upon you and be gracious to you;

the Lord lift up his countenance upon you and give you peace.

Numbers 6:24-26

Historical and Theological Significance

The role of the Levitical priesthood was to stand between God and the people of Israel. Aaron's blessing was specifically given by God as something that Aaron and his sons would speak over the people of Israel. It calls upon the Lord to shower his people with ultimate good. In a very real sense, this blessing marks the people as belonging to God and kept and protected by his power; God's face is turned away from the wicked but toward the righteous. God's peace, or *shalom* in Hebrew, is the longing and need of every human heart. Peace between God and people is the great work of redemption achieved by Christ on the cross (Ephesians 2:14-16).

Christians have been made into a royal priesthood and have every right to pronounce this blessing on others (I Peter 2:9). We pronounce it over those who *already* belong to God as a statement of *fact*; we pronounce it over those who *have yet* to receive His grace as an expression of *hope*. We ourselves embrace this blessing as our birthright and our inheritance and as a magnificent tool of ministry to others. These eternal words uttered by the eternal God Himself have brought hope and peace and comfort and illumination to millions through the ages. We should commit them to memory so we can readily bless others who desperately need God's *shalom*.

The Christ Hymn

Have this mind among yourselves, which is yours in Christ Jesus, who, though he was in the form of God, did not count equality with God a thing to be grasped, but emptied himself, by taking the form of a servant, being born in the likeness of men.

And being found in human form, he humbled himself by becoming obedient to the point of death, even death on a cross. Therefore God has highly exalted him and bestowed on him the name that is above every name, so that at the name of Jesus every knee should bow, in heaven and on earth and under the earth, and every tongue confess that Jesus Christ is Lord, to the glory of God the Father.

Philippians 2:5-11

Historical and Theological Significance

Paul's letter to the church at Philippi includes a powerful exhortation to brotherly love. In it, Paul urges Christians to take Christ as their model of humility and self-lessness. He pens a hymn which is the centerpiece of the letter and demonstrates clearly that the earliest Christians worshiped Jesus as the exalted Lord. Paul applies this rich understanding of Christ to practical issues of church life and relationships with fellow Christians.

The hymn begins by recalling Christ's place as equal to God prior to His incarnation and His willingness to empty Himself of the glories of heaven. Not only did He humble Himself by taking on human flesh, but He also became a servant who died in the most horrific of ways. His obedience and humility did not go unrewarded, for after His resurrection He was exalted and given the name that is above all names. The one who was completely humble is now the one before whom every knee will bow; the one who was degraded on the cross is now exalted as Lord of Glory. If the one true God can take on human form and endure such humiliation for our sake, surely we too can humble ourselves. This hymn teaches us the most profound things about Christ's divine nature and exalted position, but it also has the power to prompt us to true humility and service to one another.

Psalm 1

Blessed is the man
who walks not in the counsel of the wicked,
nor stands in the way of sinners,
nor sits in the seat of scoffers;
but his delight is in the law of the Lord,
and on his law he meditates day and night.

He is like a tree
planted by streams of water
that yields its fruit in its season,
and its leaf does not wither.
In all that he does, he prospers.
The wicked are not so,
but are like chaff that the wind drives away.

Therefore the wicked will not stand in the judgment,
nor sinners in the congregation of the righteous;
for the Lord knows the way of the righteous,
but the way of the wicked will perish.

Psalm 1

Historical and Theological Significance

The book of Psalms is the greatest collection of prayers, songs, and wisdom in the Bible. Its rich themes of thanks, praise, lament, and celebration have been on the hearts and lips of all worshipers of God since the days of David. Throughout the Psalms we learn that God desires his people to cry out to him, to call upon Him, to find refuge in Him. We learn that the way of the righteous is good and the way of the wicked perishes, regardless of how things may seem at times. We learn that the spiritual person can be honest with God in prayer, should humbly submit to His ways, and should stand in awe of His majesty.

The first Psalm is a fitting beginning to the book, for it draws the clear picture of the two paths: the way of the righteous and the way of the wicked. The former is like a beautiful tree growing by streams of water that is fully refreshed and sustained by God's law and is firmly established; the latter, however, is like the useless husk of the wheat that is good for nothing and ultimately blows away in the slightest of winds. This Psalm contains a clear and concise depiction of the two ways that stand before every human being. Because of this, I encourage you to memorize and recite it often as a reminder of basic spiritual realities.

Sing to the Lord

*Let the word of Christ dwell in you richly,
teaching and admonishing one another in all
wisdom, singing psalms and hymns and spiritual songs, with thankfulness in your hearts to
God.*

Colossians 3:16

God commands his people to sing to Him in worship.
This mode of expressing thanks, praise, and petition to
God is universally accessible to all human beings.
Singing is a time proven method of conveying truth,
provoking certain kinds of emotions, and stirring the
heart to adoration of God. I believe that singing a variety of songs with your family is important to worship.
To help you with this, the Family Worship Guide provides a few lists of recommended songs in Chapter
Four. The songs are divided into three categories that
correspond to the rotation of songs in the Family Worship Guide: Hymns, Devotional Songs, and Contemporary Songs. In this guide, we distinguish between the
songs in this way: ***Hymns*** are older songs that are poetic in nature, have gained wide acceptance throughout
the last several hundred years, and express deep theological truths. ***Devotional songs*** are shorter and recent,
simple and repetitive, and can have a lot of regional diversity. Sometimes these songs are referred to as "camp
songs" because they originated at church camps and are

associated with youthfulness, sincerity, and love for one another. Some devotional songs are simply Scripture put to song. ***Contemporary Songs*** are modern songs by Christian artists that have reached a degree of popularity and may be heard on the radio. An additional list of children's songs has been provided in Chapter Four. If you have young children, be sure to incorporate children's songs into your family worship, but also gradually introduce them to the rich and time-tested hymns, devotional songs, and contemporary songs. In the evangelical community, Keith and Kristin Getty are leading an exciting revival of hymn-writing and singing in church and in the home. If you aren't convinced about the value of singing for faith development, get a copy of their *Sing! How Worship Transforms your Life, Family, and your Church* (2017) and prepare to be inspired.

Tips for Singing together as a Family

1. Pick a family song for the year. Find a song that is easy to remember, has an appealing tune, and has some special meaning to the family. Sing it on a regular basis during that year (or month, quarter, or trimester – do what works for your family).

2. Invest in songbooks. Buy a songbook for every member of the family, preferably the same version your congregation uses. You can use a three-ring bindeer to hold devotional/contemporary songs that aren't in the songbook.

3. Let kids pick songs. Use the resource pages included in this guide to give children ideas for song choices.

4. Use singing resources. Singing together isn't just for the Von Trapp Family! If you aren't strong singers, consider singing along with CDs & other digital resources. YouTube is a great resource for finding encouraging and inspiring Christian hymns to sing along with. Our family listens to a lot of Praise and Harmony CDs to help us learn new music.

5. Sing, sing, sing. Be sure you sing. If singing doesn't come naturally to your family, you may be tempted to cut it out. Don't do it! Singing is a universally practiced activity that is proven to build and strengthen community. Your hearts will literally beat in rhythm while singing together. Singing helps cement truths in your children and will serve them well in the future. Sing at least one song each night no matter what, even if it's just the family song.

6. Sing with other families. Invite other Christian families over to sing together. Singing is a communal activity – practice it with other families! As a bonus, singing always sounds better with more voices, and joining with another family can give your family a sense of what it is like to experience good singing in small spaces.

Pray Always

Rejoice always, pray without ceasing, give thanks in all circumstances; for this is the will of God in Christ Jesus for you.

I Thessalonians 5:16-18

Engaging with God in prayer is fundamental to the Christian life, and prayer connects your family together spiritually. To help with this, the Family Worship Guide provides suggestions for prayer each day. The ACTS model of prayer has helped millions of people ensure their prayer life is diverse and not simply stuck in a rut of asking God for things. Following this method, each day your family will be prompted to pray a prayer of Adoration, Confession, or Thanksgiving, plus a specific kind of prayer of Supplication (intercession). For example, Monday nights call for a prayer of Adoration and a prayer of Supplication for your church family. Tuesday is a night for a prayer of Confession and Supplication for members of your immediate family. As with the other items, expand to other more personal prayer topics as needed.

Tips for Praying together

1. **Pray in order.** Pray in order – perhaps age, or maybe just where each person is sitting. You can

provide a prompt. For instance, "Thank God for something and pray for one person." Then, pray around the room in order. Our family typically starts with the youngest child and prays up the birth order, concluding with the parents.

2. **"Repeat after me" prayers.** For younger children, it's helpful to show them how to pray by using short phrases and having them repeat after you. For example, "Dear God (repeat), thank you for your love (repeat), thank you for Jesus (repeat)," etc. If Christ's disciples needed to be shown how to pray, certainly our children need to be shown as well.

3. **Use the *ACTS* method.** As noted above, one tried and true method of prayer is to follow the ACTS method: **Adoration** (themes of praise), **Confession** (themes related to confession of sin but also confession of belief), **Thanksgiving** (themes of gratefulness for specific attributes of God or blessings received), **Supplication** (themes of intercession where we ask God for our heart's desire). The Family Worship Guide schedule is designed around the ACTS model with a different prompt for intercession on each day of the week.

4. **Keep a record of prayer requests.** As a family, write down prayer requests in a journal and periodically look back to see how your prayers

were answered. These answers can be incorporated into prayers of thanksgiving.

5. **Use a church bulletin.** Most churches publish prayer requests in the bulletin. You will never run out of things to pray for if you have a bulletin at hand. Also, when it comes time to pray for church leaders, church events, etc., you will find specifics in the bulletin.

6. **Use a church directory.** When praying for the congregation, there is nothing like a church directory to help liven things up for children. It's one thing to say we need to pray for Mrs. Collins who has cancer, but it is another thing to open the directory to her picture and pray for her. Seeing the face of the person you're praying for makes prayer more personal for children.

7. **Pray for your children.** Each day pray with and for your children during family worship. Visit http://citylightomaha.org/wp-content/uploads/2014/08/31_days_prayer.pdf for a calendar that provides specific prayer prompts for each day of the month as you pray for your children.

8. **Silent prayer.** Learning to sit in silence for individual prayer is valuable. This is doable with older children, but it's difficult with younger ones. A good format is to create a silent prayer "sandwich" – have an adult pray an opening and

closing prayer with space in the middle for silent prayer.

9. **Prayer day.** Assign each person in your family a day when it's their turn to pray.

10. **"Pray individually with your children.** Develop a habit of praying privately with a different child each night (assuming you have multiple children), on the same day each week. That day will become "her day," a day that she has a few minutes of special time with mom or dad in private prayer. For example, pray with your oldest child on Mondays, your next child on Tuesdays, and so on. We've used this system to continue praying with our children all the way through college.

Resources for Family Worship

Family Worship Guides & Resources

As your family grows in the practice of family worship, you will need to adjust the format of your worship together. In the early years, when your children are small, focus on biblical knowledge, much of which is memorized and chanted together and learned through question and answer format. As they get older and begin to have more questions about the Christian life and how it must be lived out, reserve time for Bible discussion and be flexible with the plan. Remember, the goal is to spend time in God's presence as a family, giving honor and praise to His name and being instructed by His Word. Any combination of Reading, Reciting, Singing, and Praying is good, and these guides are intended to provide structure until you find your own rhythm as a family. Sometimes, family worship mainly consists of singing songs because everyone is in singing mood; other times, it might simply involve reading a portion of the Bible together, singing the Doxology, and saying a short prayer. Let the guides be just that – guides that provide some structure during a season of your family's life together in worship. Included in this chapter are several resources to help with the structure of family worship.

- Starter Kit Checklist
- Worship Guides
- Bible Discussion Questions
- Topical Discussion Questions
- Bible Reading Plans
- Snow-Day Family Worship Guide
- Songs (Hymns, Devotional Songs, Contemporary Songs, Children's Songs)
- Recitation Chart

Starter Kit Checklist

When getting started with family worship it can be helpful to have all the materials you need together in one place for easy access. Developing this material can help you be ready for consistent and meaningful gatherings in your home.

- **Bin**. Find a sturdy and aesthetically pleasing bin with a lid on it that can hold all the materials you need for family worship and be kept in a convenient place. Keep these contents in the bin.

- **Family Worship Guide**. A copy of this booklet with a bookmark on the specific guide the family is currently using.

- **Recitation Chart**. Laminated copies of the recitation chart for use when memorizing the six critical passages. When guests are present, give them a copy so they can join in when reciting the passage of the day.

- **Songbooks**. Enough songbooks for everyone in the family.

- **Bible**. A designated reading Bible.

- **Bible Story Books**. For families with small children, one or two Bible story books.

- **Bible Study Resources**. A resource like a good Bible dictionary to help with questions about Biblical topics.

- **Church Pictorial Directory**. A copy of the Church's current directory is important for intercessory prayer.

- **Prayer Journal**. A prayer journal and writing utensil.

Worship Guides

The Quarterly Guide (for those just getting started)

The Quarterly Guide is for families that are just getting started with family worship. It is designed so that each quarter your family can work to memorize one of the six foundational passages. Eventually, your family will be able to recite all of these passages by heart. Each quarter, your family will work on memorizing a different passage. After 18 months, you will have powerful biblical truth committed to memory that will become part of the family culture for generations to come. Since the Quarterly Guide allows time for memorization, the Bible reading portion of worship should be shorter. Select appropriate passages from the Old and New Testaments using one of the suggested reading plans or some other plan. The basic weekly plan for each quarter will be repeated throughout each quarter.

1st Quarter (Jan–Mar)

Day	Read the Word	Recite Truth	Sing to the Lord	Pray Always
Mon	Old Testament	Ten Commandments	Devotional Song	Prayer of Praise & Prayer for Church Family
Tues	New Testament	Ten Commandments	Hymn	Prayer of Confession & Prayer for Immediate Family
Wed	Old Testament	Ten Commandments	Contemporary Song	Prayer of Thanksgiving & Prayer for neighbors and friends
Thurs	New Testament	Ten Commandments	Hymn	Prayer of Praise & Prayer for extended family
Fri	New Testament	Ten Commandments	Contemporary Song	Prayer of Confession & Prayer for Missionaries and Evangelism
Sat	Old Testament	Ten Commandments	Devotional Song	Prayer of Thanksgiving and for Church Leadership

The Ten Commandments

1. I am the Lord your God, who brought you out of Egypt, out of the land of slavery. You shall have no other gods before me.

2. You shall not make for yourself an idol in the form of anything in heaven above or on the earth beneath or in the waters below. You shall not bow down to them or worship them.

3. You shall not misuse the name of the Lord your God, for the Lord will not hold anyone guiltless who misuses his name.

4. Remember the Sabbath day by keeping it holy. Six days you shall labor and do all your work, but the seventh day is a sabbath to the Lord your God.

5. Honor your father and your mother, so that you may live long in the land the Lord your God is giving you.

6. You shall not murder.

7. You shall not commit adultery.

8. You shall not steal.

9. You shall not bear false testimony against your neighbor.

10. You shall not covet anything that belongs to your neighbor.

New International Version, 1984

2nd Quarter (Apr–June)

Day	Read the Word	Recite Truth	Sing to the Lord	Pray Always
Mon	Old Testament	The Lord's Prayer	Devotional Song	Prayer of Praise & Prayer for Church Family
Tues	New Testament	The Lord's Prayer	Hymn	Prayer of Confession & Prayer for Immediate Family
Wed	Old Testament	The Lord's Prayer	Contemporary Song	Prayer of Thanksgiving & Prayer for neighbors and friends
Thurs	New Testament	The Lord's Prayer	Hymn	Prayer of Praise & Prayer for extended family
Fri	New Testament	The Lord's Prayer	Contemporary Song	Prayer of Confession & Prayer for Missionaries and Evangelism
Sat	Old Testament	The Lord's Prayer	Devotional Song	Prayer of Thanksgiving and for Church Leadership

The Lord's Prayer

Our Father in heaven, hallowed be your name.

Your kingdom come,
 your will be done, on earth as it is in heaven.
Give us this day our daily bread,
and forgive us our debts,
    as we also have forgiven our debtors.
And lead us not into temptation,
    but deliver us from evil.

For yours is the kingdom, and the power,

and the glory, forever.

Amen

Matthew 6:9-13 ESV

3rd Quarter (July – Sept)

Day	Read the Word	Recite Truth	Sing to the Lord	Pray Always
Mon	Old Testament	The Ancient Confession	Devotional Song	Prayer of Praise & Prayer for Church Family
Tues	New Testament	The Ancient Confession	Hymn	Prayer of Confession & Prayer for Immediate Family
Wed	Old Testament	The Ancient Confession	Contemporary Song	Prayer of Thanksgiving & Prayer for neighbors and friends
Thurs	New Testament	The Ancient Confession	Hymn	Prayer of Praise & Prayer for extended family
Fri	New Testament	The Ancient Confession	Contemporary Song	Prayer of Confession & Prayer for Missionaries and Evangelism
Sat	Old Testament	The Ancient Confession	Devotional Song	Prayer of Thanksgiving and for Church Leadership

The Ancient Confession

I believe in God the Father Almighty, the Creator of Heaven and Earth

And in Jesus Christ his only son, our Lord

Who was conceived of the Holy Spirit, born of the Virgin Mary, suffered under Pontius Pilate, was crucified, died, and was buried

The third day He arose again from the dead. He ascended into heaven and sits at the right hand of God the Father Almighty, whence He shall come to judge the living and the dead.

I believe in the Holy Spirit, the Holy universal Church, the communion of saints, the forgiveness of sin, the resurrection of the body, and in life everlasting, Amen.

4ᵗʰ Quarter (Oct – Dec)

Day	Read the Word	Recite Truth	Sing to the Lord	Pray Always
Mon	Old Testament	Aaron's Blessing	Devotional Song	Prayer of Praise & Prayer for Church Family
Tues	New Testament	Aaron's Blessing	Hymn	Prayer of Confession & Prayer for Immediate Family
Wed	Old Testament	Aaron's Blessing	Contemporary Song	Prayer of Thanksgiving & Prayer for neighbors and friends
Thurs	New Testament	Aaron's Blessing	Hymn	Prayer of Praise & Prayer for extended family
Fri	New Testament	Aaron's Blessing	Contemporary Song	Prayer of Confession & Prayer for Missionaries and Evangelism
Sat	Old Testament	Aaron's Blessing	Devotional Song	Prayer of Thanksgiving and for Church Leadership

Aaron's Blessing

The Lord bless you and keep you;

the Lord make his face to shine upon you and be gracious to you;

the Lord lift up his countenance upon you and give you peace.

Numbers 6:24-26 ESV

Year 2-1st Quarter (Jan-Mar)

Day	Read the Word	Recite Truth	Sing to the Lord	Pray Always
Mon	Old Testament	The Christ Hymn	Devotional Song	Prayer of Praise & Prayer for Church Family
Tues	New Testament	The Christ Hymn	Hymn	Prayer of Confession & Prayer for Immediate Family
Wed	Old Testament	The Christ Hymn	Contemporary Song	Prayer of Thanksgiving & Prayer for neighbors and friends
Thurs	New Testament	The Christ Hymn	Hymn	Prayer of Praise & Prayer for extended family
Fri	New Testament	The Christ Hymn	Contemporary Song	Prayer of Confession & Prayer for Missionaries and Evangelism
Sat	Old Testament	The Christ Hymn	Devotional Song	Prayer of Thanksgiving and for Church Leadership

The Christ Hymn

Have this mind among yourselves, which is yours in Christ Jesus, who, though he was in the form of God, did not count equality with God a thing to be grasped, but emptied himself, by taking the form of a servant, being born in the likeness of men.

And being found in human form, he humbled himself by becoming obedient to the point of death, even death on a cross. Therefore God has highly exalted him and bestowed on him the name that is above every name, so that at the name of Jesus every knee should bow, in heaven and on earth and under the earth, and every tongue confess that Jesus Christ is Lord, to the glory of God the Father.

Philippians 2:5-11 ESV

Year 2-2nd Quarter (Apr-Jun)

Day	Read the Word	Recite Truth	Sing to the Lord	Pray Always
Mon	Old Testament	Blessed is the Man	Devotional Song	Prayer of Praise & Prayer for Church Family
Tues	New Testament	Blessed is the Man	Hymn	Prayer of Confession & Prayer for Immediate Family
Wed	Old Testament	Blessed is the Man	Contemporary Song	Prayer of Thanksgiving & Prayer for neighbors and friends
Thurs	New Testament	Blessed is the Man	Hymn	Prayer of Praise & Prayer for extended family
Fri	New Testament	Blessed is the Man	Contemporary Song	Prayer of Confession & Prayer for Missionaries and Evangelism
Sat	Old Testament	Blessed is the Man	Devotional Song	Prayer of Thanksgiving and for Church Leadership

Blessed is the Man

Blessed is the man who walks not in the counsel of the
wicked,

nor stands in the way of sinners, nor sits in the seat
of scoffers;

but his delight is in the law of the Lord, and on
his law he meditates day and night.

He is like a tree planted by streams of water

that yields its fruit in its season, and its leaf does not
wither.

In all that he does, he prospers.

The wicked are not so, but are like chaff that the
wind drives away.

Therefore the wicked will not stand in the judgment,

nor sinners in the congregation of the righteous;

for the Lord knows the way of the righteous,

but the way of the wicked will perish.

Psalm 1 (ESV)

The Weekly Guide
(for those further along the way)

The Weekly Guide is designed for families that have established a regular rhythm of family worship but still need some structure. It's designed so that each week the family focuses on the Bible reading and spends time discussing the passages or general topics of concern to the Christian life (see question lists below). This pattern of family worship helps the family talk openly about the Bible and its application to life. Since the family has already memorized the six foundational passages, these passages are simply recited on the corresponding evening with little or no discussion.

Weekly Worship Guide

Day	Read the Word	Recite Truth	Sing to the Lord	Pray Always
Mon	Old Testament (Bible Discussion)	The Ten Commandments	Hymn	Prayer of Praise & Prayer for Church Family
Tues	New Testament (Topical discussion)	The Ancient Confession	Devotional Song	Prayer of Confession & Prayer for Immediate Family
Wed	Old Testament (Open forum)	The Lord's Prayer	Contemporary Song	Prayer of Thanksgiving & Prayer for neighbors and friends
Thurs	New Testament (Bible Discussion)	Aaron's Blessing	Hymn	Prayer of Praise & Prayer for extended family
Fri	New Testament (Open forum)	Hymn of the Christ	Devotional Song	Prayer of Confession & Prayer for Missionaries and Evangelism
Sat	Old Testament (Topical discussion)	Blessed is the Man	Contemporary Song	Prayer of Thanksgiving and for Church Leadership

Discussion Questions

Bible Discussion

Discussing the Bible as a family is a rewarding experience. Sometimes the discussion may get deep and hinge on technical information that can be found in a good study Bible, commentary, or Bible dictionary. Other times, the emphasis is more personal and focused on individual application of the Bible. Below are some basic questions that can be helpful when discussing the Bible together as a family.

Interpretation Questions:

1. What is the historical setting of the passage?

2. When & where was this passage written?

3. Who wrote this passage and what was the original audience?

4. What seems to be the purpose of the passage?

5. What is the literary context of the passage? Is it poetry, history, law, prophetic, or song? How might that affect our understanding of the passage?

6. What is the overall message of the passage?

7. How does the passage uniquely speak to the original readers?

8. How does the passage speak to people in every age?

General Application Questions:

1. What does the passage say about God and his nature or character?

2. What does the passage say about humanity and its condition?

3. What does the passage say about God's people?

4. How would our lives change if we followed the teaching of this passage?

Personal Application Questions:

In this passage...

1. Does this passage mention a sin that we need to confess or forsake?

2. Does this passage give a command that we should obey?

3. Does this passage make a promise that we can look to in our current life?

4. Does this passage have a prayer that we can pray?

5. Does this passage include a promise that we need to hold on to?

Topical Discussion

Children have lots of questions about the Christian faith and family worship provides a great place to discuss them. Often, these questions are about practices or traditions of the Church and other times they are life questions raised at school, on the sports field, or in media. Topics will arise naturally based on the things going on in your children's lives, but other times, it can be helpful to raise questions and ask kids how they would answer them. Below are thirty sample questions that might be worth discussing in family worship. Use these as ideas and develop your own list of questions to work through with your family.

1. Why did God create the world?

2. Why do we pray before meals?

3. Do pets go to heaven?

4. Why do we go to church on Sunday?

5. Does God sleep or need rest?

6. Are [a specific religious group] Christians?

7. Why did God make people?

8. Why do bad things happen to good people?

9. What happens to us when we die?

10. How do we know if we are too busy?

11. Is Jesus God?

12. Why do we partake of communion every Sunday?

13. How much should I give to the Lord?

14. Why do some people die when they are not old?

15. How do we know when our clothing is modest or not?

16. What is Heaven like?

17. What are valid reasons to miss a Sunday worship assembly?

18. What does God look like?

19. How do we know we have the right religion?

20. Who created God?

21. How do we know that Bible can be trusted?

22. How can we share our faith without being too "pushy"?

23. Does God have a friend or is he alone?

24. Why can't we see God?

25. Why do we worship the way we do?

26. Why does God love people?

27. Why do we pray in Jesus' name?

28. How do we know that certain words are cussing or swearing?

29. Is it wrong to marry a non-Christian?

30. Why do we close our eyes to pray?

Bible Reading Plans

Many different Bible reading plans are available on the internet and in good study Bibles. Do some research and find a plan that fits your family's needs. Below is a list of five good *kinds* of reading plans, as well as two *specific examples* of Bible reading plans.

1. Psalms and Proverbs. Reading the Psalms and Proverbs are essential for family worship. Psalms provides the language of prayer and worship. Proverbs is good for training children in the basics of wisdom and prudent living.

2. Entire Bible plans. These plans are designed for the long haul and can take quite a while to read as a family. Keep in mind that reading large chunks of the Bible at a sitting may be difficult for small (or older) children.

3. Survey of the Bible. Survey plans pick out key passages, giving readers an overview of the big picture of the Bible. I recommend using a survey or sampler approach to the Bible for family worship and using whole Bible reading plans for individual study.

4. Focused Reading. This method seeks to read straight through portions of Scripture, one book at a time. For example, the family might read slowly through the Epistle of James for a month and include time for discussion along the way. You could decide together what portion of Scripture to read next.

5. Classic Passages. There are certain passages of scripture that have gone down as classics and form some of the language of the Christian faith.

Example 1
Survey of the Bible Reading Plan

Old Testament Survey Readings	New Testament Survey Readings
Genesis 1-3, 12, 15, 22	Matthew 1-2, 5-7
Exodus 1-5, 12-14, 20	Matthew 17, 26-28
Leviticus 1, 10, 16, 25	Mark 1-4, 10, 15-16
Numbers 3-4, 6, 11-14	Luke 1-2, 4-6
Deuteronomy 5-8, 28-31, 34	Luke 8-10, 22-24
Joshua 1-6, 23-24	John 1, 3-4
Judges 1-4, 13-16	John 13-17, 19-21
Ruth 1-4	Acts 1-4
1 Samuel 7-10, 12, 15-20, 28, 31	Acts 8-10, 12-15
2 Samuel 5-8, 11-13, 15, 18	Romans 5-8, 12
1 Kings 3, 6-12, 17-19, 21	1 Corinthians 1-2, 13
2 Kings 1-2, 6-7, 11-12, 17-23	2 Corinthians 4-5, 8-9
1 Chronicles 15-17, 21-22, 28-29	Galatians 5-6
2 Chronicles 5-10, 14-16, 24-26, 29-35	Ephesians 4-6
Ezra 3, 6-7	Philippians 2, 4
Nehemiah 1-2, 4, 6	Colossians 1, 4
Esther 1-4	1 Thessalonians 2, 4 and 2 Thessalonians 3
Job 1-3, 38-42	1 Timothy 1, 3

Psalms 1, 8, 19, 23, 51, 100, 103, 139	2 Timothy 3-4
Proverbs 1-3	Titus 2 and Philemon
Ecclesiastes 1-5, 12 and Songs 1-2	Hebrews 10-13
Isaiah 1-2, 6, 40, 52-55	James 1-3
Jeremiah 1-5 and Lamentations 3	1 Peter 1, 5 and 2 Peter 1
Ezekiel 1-3, 18, 33	1 John 1-2, 2 John, and 3 John
Daniel 1-2, 4-6	Jude, Revelation 19-22
Hosea 1-4 and Joel 2	
Amos 3, Obadiah, and Jonah 1	
Micah 1-2 and Nahum 1	
Habakkuk 1, Zephaniah 3, Haggai	
Zechariah 1-2 and Malachi 1	

* Reading the material in this chart will enable you and your family to engage with the highlights from each book of the Bible. Adapted from https://www.biblegateway.com/reading-plans/survey.

Example 2
50 Classic Bible Passages

Passage	Subject	Passage	Subject
1. John 3:16-17	God so loved the world	26. Genesis 1:1-2	In the Beginning
2. John 1:1-	In the beginning was the Word	27. Luke 1:46-55	My soul magnifies the Lord
3. Proverbs 3:5-6	He will make straight your paths	28. Romans 8:35-39	More than conquerors
4. Romans 12:1-2	Be transformed by the renewing of your mind	29. I Corinthians 13:4-7	Love is patient, love is kind…
5. Galatians 5:22-23	The Fruit of the Spirit	30. Ephesians 6:10-17	Full Armor of God
6. Hebrews 12:1	A great cloud of witnesses	31. Philippians 4:6-8	Peace of God
7. 2 Timothy 3:16-17	All scripture is God-Breathed	32. I John 4:7-12	God is Love
8. Acts 2:36-41	Repent and be baptized	33. Joshua 24:15	As for me and My house
9. Acts 2:42-47	They devoted themselves	34. Jeremiah 31:31-34	The new Covenant
10. Acts 4:12	There is no other name	35. Luke 2:10-11	Good news of great joy

11. Jeremiah 29:11	I know the plans I have for you, declares the Lord	36. Malachi 1:11	Great is the name of the LORD
12. James 1:2-3	Consider it all joy	37. I John 1:8-9	God is faithful and just
13. Matthew 5:3-12	Blessed are the…	38. Mark 8:34	Take up your cross and follow me
14. Lamentations 3:21-23	The Steadfast love of the Lord	39. Colossians 3:1	Seek the Things Above
15. Psalm 19:14	Let the words of my mouth	40. Revelation 4:8	Holy, Holy, Holy
16. Deuteronomy 6:4-5	Hear o Israel	41. Isaiah 57:15	I dwell in a high and holy place
17. John 1:14	And the Word became flesh	42. Psalm 121:1-8	I lift up my eyes to the hills
18. Proverbs 17:9	Whoever covers an offense seeks love	43. Genesis 1:27-28	In his own image
19. Matthew 28:19-20	Go and make disciples	44. Genesis 12:1-3	I will make you a great nation
20. I John 1:7	If we walk in the light	45. Job 1:21	Blessed be the name of the Lord

21. Revelation 5:9-10	By your blood you ransomed a people for God	46. Proverbs 16:24	Pleasants words are a honeycomb
22. Psalm 117	Praise the Lord	47. Proverbs 6:16-19	Six things the Lord hates
23. Isaiah 9:6-7	Birth of the Messiah	48. Micah 6:8	Walk humbly with your God
24. Isaiah 53:4-9	Suffering Servant	49. Zephaniah 3:17	The Lord is with You
25. Joshua 1:9	Strong and Courageous	50. Psalm 78:1-4	Tell the next generation

Snow Day Sunday Family Worship

During the winter, Sunday worship assemblies are occasionally cancelled due to inclement weather. But it's still the Lord's Day, a time to pause for reflection, worship, and instruction. Below is an example of what a family could do on a Sunday Snow Day. As with everything in the guide, allow this example to prompt your own thinking and adapt as needed.

Snow Day In-Home Family Worship

Prayer of Praise & Thanks (reflect on blessings, share them with one another and thank God for them)

Sing: *"When Upon Life's Billows" (Count Your Blessings) & "Thank You, Lord" (For all that you've done). Look up lyrics on the internet or use a hymnbook if you have one.*

Read Psalm 34 and reflect on the goodness of God.

Sing: *"You Have Been Good"* & *"Unto Thee, O Lord"* & *"For the Beauty of the Earth."*

Reflect on the gospel of Jesus Christ by reading these passages:

- I Corinthians 15:1-11
- II Corinthians 5:11-21

Sing: *"O Sacred Head"* & *"In Christ Alone"* & *"Here I am to Worship"*

Communion. If appropriate, prepare the bread and cup and conduct a communion remembrance. Read I Corinthians 11:17-32 and reflect on the Lord's death until he comes.

Prayer of Intercession

- Read today's bulletin (if available online) and pray for members in need. Pray for others you know of who are sick and hurting. Pray for the lost in your neighborhood, in your family, in your circle of friends. Pray that God will open a door for you to share Christ with them. Pray for our congregation and the new Christians in our midst who have been baptized recently. Pray for...

Fellowship

- Look over the bulletin or church website and plan to attend the upcoming events that will strengthen you in Christ and connect you more deeply with other Christians.

- Call to at least one other church member and visit. See how their week went and maybe even exchange prayer requests. Text at least 5 people from church to wish them a great Lord's Day!

Songs

Classic Hymns

Below is a list of classic hymns our family has enjoyed singing. Song numbers correspond to *The Songs of Faith and Praise*, ed. Alton H. Howard (1994/1998).

1. A Wonderful Savior (#508)

2. Abide with me (#808)

3. Alas and did my savior bleed (#324)

4. All hail the power of Jesus name (#145)

5. All to Jesus I surrender (#662)

6. Amazing Grace (#129)

7. Be still my soul (#689)

8. Be thou my vision

9. Be with me Lord (#778)

10. Because He lives (#464)

11. Blessed assurance Jesus is Mine (#480)

12. Blest be the tie that binds (#711)

13. Come let us all unite to sing (#121)

14. Come Thou Fount of Every Blessing (#226)

15. Come we that love the Lord (#869)

16. Count your blessings (#742)

17. Dear Lord and Father of Mankind (#770)

18. Did you think to pray? (#848)

19. Doxology (Praise God from Whom all blessings flow) (#66)

20. Emmanuel, Emmanuel (#164)

21. Fairest Lord Jesus (#288)

22. Faith is the victory (#469)

23. Farther along (#753)

24. Father hear the prayer we offer (#777)

25. For the Beauty of the Earth (#67)

26. Freely, Freely (#635)

27. Gentle Shepherd (#845)

28. God be with you till we meet again (#755)

29. God is the Fountain Whence (#117)

30. Great is thy faithfulness (#57)

31. Guide me oh thou Great Jehovah (#390)

Songs

32. Hallelujah Praise Jehovah (#3)

33. Hallelujah What a Savior (Man of sorrows) (#337)

34. Have thine own way Lord (#552)

35. He gave me a song (#608)

36. He lives (#346)

37. He's my king (#166)

38. Heavenly Sunlight (#611)

39. Holy, Holy, Holy (#47)

40. How Firm A Foundation (#457)

41. How Great thou art (#76)

42. I come to the garden alone (#595)

43. I have decided to follow Jesus (#674)

44. I need thee every hour (#837)

45. I walk with the King (#550)

46. I'll fly away (#851)

47. I'm not ashamed to own my Lord (#609)

48. In Heavenly Love Abiding (#139)

49. In loving kindness Jesus came (#504)

50. It is well with my soul (#490)

51. Jesus is coming soon (#712)

52. Jesus Keep me near the cross (#383)

53. Jesus, Lover of my soul (#807)

54. Just as I am (#924)

55. Lead me gently home father (#823)

56. Living by Faith (#560)

57. Lord we come before thee now (#797)

58. Love Lifted me (#453)

59. Love one another (Angry Words) (#719)

60. Master the Tempest is Raging (#189)

61. More love to Thee o Christ (#700)

62. My Hope is Built on Nothing Else (#538)

63. My Jesus I love Thee (#701)

64. Nearer my God to thee (#684)

65. Nearer still nearer (#478)

66. Nothing but the blood (#902)

67. Now the day is over (#795)

68. Oh How I love Jesus (#574)

69. Oh Sacred Head (#318)

70. On Zion's Glorious Summit (#227)

71. Open my eyes that I may see (#830)

72. Our God He is Alive (#23)

73. Ring out the Message (#622)

74. Send the Light (#650)

75. Sing to me of heaven (#716)

76. Softly and tenderly (#934)

77. Sweet Hour of Prayer (#827)

78. Sweet Will of God (#822)

79. Take time to be Holy (#731)

80. Teach me thy way Oh Lord (#762)

81. Ten Thousand Angels (#349)

82. The Glory Land Way (#535)

83. The Lord's My Shepherd (#393)

84. The Old Rugged Cross (#313)

85. There is a Balm in Gilead (#961)

86. There is a habitation (#860)

87. There is Power in the Blood (#903)

88. Tis so sweet to trust in Jesus (#674)

89. To Canaan's land I'm on my way (#867)

90. Trust and Obey (#915)

91. Victory in Jesus (#470)

92. We Praise thee Oh God (#2)

93. We're marching to Zion (#869)

94. What a friend we have in Jesus (#800)

95. When I survey the wondrous cross (#315)

96. When my love to Christ Grows weak (#350)

97. When the Roll is Called up Yonder (#852)

98. When we all get to heaven (#853)

99. Why did my savior come to earth? (#382)

100. Will you not tell it today? (#628)

Devotional Songs

As mentioned above, devotional songs have a lot of regional diversity. Below are some devotional songs well-loved in our region of the country.

1. A common love

2. Above all else

3. Ain't no Rock

4. All in All

5. As the deer

6. Awesome God

7. Be still and know

8. Bind us together

9. Blue skies and rainbows

10. Break my heart

11. Clap, Clap Your hands

12. Come, Now is the time to worship

13. Day by Day, you reveal your love to me

14. Days of Elijah

15. Faithful Love

16. Father God (may my steps be worship)

17. Father I adore you

18. Firm foundation

19. For all that you've done I will thank you

20. Get right Church

21. Glorify Thy Name

22. Good to me

23. Have you seen Jesus my Lord

24. He has made me glad

25. He is able

26. Hide me Away, O Lord

27. Highest Place

28. Holy Lord

29. Hosanna

30. How deep the Father's Love

31. Humble yourself

32. I Am (Light of day…)

33. I Cry out

34. I exalt Thee

35. I love the Lord Messiah

36. I love you Lord

37. I Stand in Awe

38. I want Jesus to walk with me

39. I want to know Christ

40. I will call upon the Lord

41. I will never be the same again

42. I will serve you

43. Instruments of your peace

44. Into your courts

45. It only takes a spark (Pass it on)

46. Jesus is Able

47. Jesus is Lord

48. Jesus, Let us come to Know you

49. Jesus, Name above of all names

50. King of Kings and Lord of Lords

51. Kumbayah

52. Let us Worship

53. Let your Spirit come

54. Light the fire

55. Listen to our hearts

56. Lord I lift you name on high

57. Lord Listen to your children praying

58. Lord my desire

59. Lord Reign in Me

60. Lord the people praise you

61. Lord, be there for me when I fall

62. Make me a servant

63. Marvelous things

64. My Eyes are dry

65. My God Reigns (There's nowhere else that I'd rather be…)

66. My only hope is you Jesus

67. Oh I was made for this

68. Oh Lord our Lord How majestic is Your Name

69. Oh Lord You're beautiful

70. On Bended Knee

71. Our God Reigns

72. Pierce my Ear

73. Rejoice in the Lord Always

74. Restore my spirit Lord

75. Sanctuary

76. Seek Ye First

77. Shout Hallelujah

78. Sing Hallelujah to the Lord

79. Someday

80. Soon and very soon

81. Step by Step

82. Take Control

83. Take my life (Holiness…)

84. Tears of the Lamb

85. Thank you Lord for loving me

86. The battle belongs to the Lord

87. The Greatest Commands

88. The Reason I live in this world

89. The steadfast love of the Lord

90. There is a redeemer

91. There's a stirring

92. This is day

93. Unto Thee oh Lord

94. We are standing on Holy Ground

95. We bow down

96. We exalt thee

97. We will glorify the King of Kings

98. What a mighty God we serve

99. You are the song that I sing

100. Your love is Amazing (Hallelujah)

Contemporary Songs

By their nature contemporary songs are constantly changing. Below are some contemporary songs that could be sung in family worship. Find lyrics on the internet or sing along on Youtube.

1. Ancient Words

2. Awesome God

3. Be strong and courageous

4. Beautiful Lamb

5. Beautiful one

6. Better than Life

7. Blessed be your Name

8. Christ Above Me

9.   Christ is Risen from the Dead

10. Come as you are

11. Cornerstone

12. God has smiled on me

13. He is Able

14. He will come and save

15. Here I am to worship

16. His forever (Jesus friend of sinners)

17. Hosanna

18. How Deep the Father's Love for Us

19. I will be still and know you are God

20. I Will Rise

21. In Christ alone

22. Inside out my soul cries out

23. Let God Arise

24. Lord Reign in Me

25. Lord, Take control

26. Mighty to Save

27. Oceans

28. Oh the Blood

29. Only by Grace

30. Praise be to the Lord

31. Rescue me

32. Rock of Ages

33. Salvation belongs to our God

34. Shine Jesus Shine

35. Shout Hallelujah

36. Shout to the North

37. Stronger

38. Surround us Lord

39. Ten Thousand Reasons

40. That's why we praise him

41. Walking in the light

42. Water you turned into wine

43. We will worship the Lamb of Glory

44. What the Lord has done in me

45. Wonderful merciful Savior

46. You are good

47. You are there

48. I lay me down

Classic Children's Songs

Here is a list of fun kids songs that have instilled a love of singing in many kids and often get them moving.

1. Blue Skies and Rainbows

2. Deep and Wide

3. Father Abraham

4. Fruit of the Spirit

5. Fuzzy Caterpillar

6. Give me oil for my lamp

7. He's got the whole world in His hand

8. He's still working on me

9. Hippopotamus song

10. I am a C H R I S T I A N

11. I'm in the Lord's Army

12. I've got confidence

13. I've Got Joy down in my heart

14. I've got peace like a river

15. Jesus Loves me this I know

16. Jesus Loves the little children

17. Love is something if you give it away

18. My God is so Big

19. Oh be careful little eyes what you see

20. Only a boy named David

21. Peter and John went to pray

22. Praise Ye the Lord

23. Rejoice in the Lord Always

24. Rise and Shine (arky, arky)

25. Roll the gospel chariot along

26. The B I B L E

27. The Wise man built his house upon the Rock

28. There's a Sea of Galilee

29. This little light of mine

30. Twelve Men went to spy on Canaan

31. Who made the bugs to jump?

32. Who's that walkin on the Water?

33. Zacchaeus was a wee little man

Recitation Chart

Make copies and use when reciting & memorizing, or when visitors are present.

The Ten Commandments

1. I am the Lord your God, who brought you out of Egypt, out of the land of slavery. You shall have no other gods before me.

2. You shall not make for yourself an idol in the form of anything in heaven above or on the earth beneath or in the waters below. You shall not bow down to them or worship them.

3. You shall not misuse the name of the Lord your God, for the Lord will not hold anyone guiltless who misuses his name.

4. Remember the Sabbath day by keeping it holy. Six days you shall labor and do all your work, but the seventh day is a sabbath to the Lord your God.

5. Honor your father and your mother, so that you may live long in the land the Lord your God is giving you.

6. You shall not murder.

7. You shall not commit adultery.

8. You shall not steal.

9. You shall not bear false testimony against your neighbor.

10. You shall not covet anything that belongs to your neighbor.

Abridged, New International Version, 1984

The Lord's Prayer

Our Father in heaven, hallowed be your name.

Your kingdom come, your will be done, on earth as it is in heaven.

Give us this day our daily bread, and forgive us our debts, as we also have forgiven our debtors.

And lead us not into temptation,but deliver us from evil.

For yours is the kingdom, and the power,and the glory, forever.Amen

Matthew 6:9-13 ESV

The Ancient Confession

I believe in God the Father Almighty, the Creator of Heaven and Earth

And in Jesus Christ his only son, our Lord

Who was conceived of the Holy Spirit, born of the Virgin Mary, suffered under Pontius Pilate, was crucified, died, and was buried

The third day He arose again from the dead.

He ascended into heaven and sits at the right hand of God the Father Almighty, whence He shall come to judge the living and the dead

I believe in the Holy Spirit, the Holy universal Church, the communion of saints, the forgiveness of sin, the resurrection of the body, and in life everlasting, Amen

Aaron's Blessing

The Lord bless you and keep you;

the Lord make his face to shine upon you and be gracious to you;

the Lord lift up his countenance upon you and give you peace.

Numbers 6:24-26 ESV

The Christ Hymn

Have this mind among yourselves, which is yours in Christ Jesus, who, though he was in the form of God, did not count equality with God a thing to be grasped, but emptied himself, by taking the form of a servant, being born in the likeness of men.

And being found in human form, he humbled himself by becoming obedient to the point of death, even death on a cross.

Therefore God has highly exalted him and bestowed on him the name that is above every name, so that at the name of Jesus every knee should bow, in heaven and on earth and under the earth, and every tongue confess that Jesus Christ is Lord, to the glory of God the Father.

Philippians 2:5-11 ESV

Blessed is the Man

Blessed is the man
        who walks not in the counsel of the wicked,
    nor stands in the way of sinners,

nor sits in the seat of scoffers;
but his delight is in the law of the Lord,
and on his law he meditates day and night.
He is like a tree
planted by streams of water
that yields its fruit in its season,
and its leaf does not wither.
In all that he does, he prospers.
The wicked are not so,
but are like chaff that the wind drives away.
Therefore the wicked will not stand in the judgment,
nor sinners in the congregation of the righteous;
for the Lord knows the way of the righteous,
but the way of the wicked will perish.

Psalm 1 ESV

About the Author

Darren T. Williamson is a native of the Pacific Northwest who has ministered in churches for nearly thirty years, most recently as the Preaching Minister for the Keizer Church of Christ, Keizer, Oregon. Prior to coming to Keizer he served as minister for churches in Portland, British Columbia, and Texas. Over the years he has taught as an instructor at several Christian Universities and community colleges, including Cascade College before its closing in 2009. He is the founding director of the Campbell Institute for Theological Education. Darren holds a BA in Biblical Languages, MS in Biblical and Related Studies, MA in History, & PhD in History. He is fascinated and inspired by followers of Christ throughout history, especially during the sixteenth-century Protestant Reformation. Most importantly, Darren is a serious disciple of Jesus, devoted husband to his wife of twenty-nine years, and loving father to eight wonderful children.

If you enjoyed this book, please consider leaving an online review.
The author would appreciate reading your thoughts.

You can also follow the author on his Facebook page at:
https://www.facebook.com/Darren-T-
Williamson-132433214981625

About the Publisher

Sulis International Press publishes select fiction and nonfiction in a variety of genres under four imprints: Riversong Books, Sulis Academic Press, Sulis Press, and Keledei Publications.

For more, visit the website at
https://sulisinternational.com

Subscribe to the newsletter at
https://sulisinternational.com/subscribe/

Follow on social media

https://www.facebook.com/SulisInternational
https://twitter.com/Sulis_Intl
https://www.pinterest.com/Sulis_Intl/
https://www.instagram.com/sulis_international/

Made in United States
Orlando, FL
16 February 2022

14874608R00093